when
godly
robes
unravel

when godly robes unravel

randall massie

COLLEGE PRESS PUBLISHING CO., Joplin, Missouri

dedication

To my loving parents, Russell and Sarah Massie.
The example of your faith in word and deed
led me to make Jesus my Lord.
Thanks for standing by me all the way.

TABLE OF CONTENTS

acknowledgements

My deepest thanks to:

Terry Rush for his suggestions and encouragement;
Arthur Rawlings for the use of his computer and for his proof-reading skill;
My loving wife, Fran, who worked nearly as hard as I did on this book;
And to the Jacksonville, Illinois, Church of Christ for helping me grow over the last seven years.

introduction

Why should I read this book?

Considering the sheer volume of religious literature available today this question deserves prime consideration. Let me assure you that this book is not for everybody. If you're content with your spirituality then close the cover and put this book down. If, however, you're dissatisfied and disillusioned by conventional Christianity and crave a Spirit-filled walk with Christ then read on.

In order for a pool to remain a viable water source it must occasionally be stirred or stagnation will occur. Minds, too, must constantly be stirred to remain fresh. Faith needs occasional stirring or it too will stagnate and harden.

Second-hand faith isn't fresh faith. Vibrant faith is a personal faith. Such a faith can be yours if you question, search, examine and meditate upon *what* you believe in and in *whom* you believe. Faith is internalized through this process of serious soul searching.

Introspection is never an easy task. One extreme ignores

it altogether, while another extreme gets paralysis from analysis. Yet introspection is what this book is all about. Just remember, balance is the key.

You'll be asked to consider the concept of idolatry. You'll be confronted with questions like: Does my heart find its delight in God? Do I look to Him for all my happiness? Am I vainly trying to serve two Masters? The answers of which are known only to you — and your Father.

Those who desire holiness are willing to ask such prying, pertinent questions. Since they've found a friend in Jesus, they'll gladly tear all the idols from their hearts. But first, those idols must be detected and identified.

That's why I've written this book.

Randall L. Massie

1

hindrances to holiness

In our attempt to restore the ancient faith we often confer upon the early church a pristine purity she did not possess. Despite the pattern, the early saints struggled with everyday holiness. They possessed the right form of doctrine but fell short in its application. This tension between form and practice is clearly seen throughout the New Testament. For example, John's seven letters to the churches of Asia were written to congregations, who, on the most part, were failing to reflect Jesus in their daily lives. Paul wrote to various congregations to correct errors not only in doctrine, but in morality and living as well.

A believer named Tertullian wrote concerning the worldliness of the church of his day. Tertullian wrote at the close of the second century about 190 A.D. He attributed the worldliness he witnessed in the church to idolatry.

> The principal crime of the human race, the highest guilt charged upon the world, the whole procuring cause of judgment, is idolatry.[1]

He went on to explain that idolatry is fraud. It's refusing to give God the honor due Him and conferring that honor upon another. The result of such behavior is worldliness. When this happens, the focus of our faith is redirected and, therefore, our progress in holiness is seriously hindered.

Don't be deceived into thinking that idolatry is a problem limited to underdeveloped, third-world countries. Idolatry's threat and practice exists at this moment in our highly advanced technological society. Idolatry is not confined to those whom we call pagan. Many in our culture who are born of water and Spirit continue to unconsciously carry their idols with them into the body of Christ.

Neither was idolatry restricted to the Old Testament dispensation. New Testament saints grappled with this sin. Paul encouraged the Christians in Corinth to "flee from idolatry" (I Cor. 10:14). The beloved apostle John wrote a few decades later and reminded his children in the faith to: "keep yourselves from idols" (I John 5:21).

Both Old Testament prophet and New Testament apostle warned God's people about the influence of idolatry. That insidious influence still persists to this day.

DEFINITION

The Greek word translated idol is *eidolon*. Although *eidolon* is used to render some 15 Hebrew terms in the Septuagint, it refers without exception to the images of heathen gods.[2] The word *eidolon* (idol) comes from the Greek word *eidos* which means an appearance or that which is seen. *Eidolon* is used to mean any unsubstantial form such as the image reflected in a mirror or on a pond. An idol, therefore, was something that appeals to the senses but has no substantial reality in and of itself.

God's prohibition concerning idols is found in the Decalogue. In the third month following their miraculous release from Egyptian slavery, Moses led the children of Israel to the foot of Mount Sinai. Here, Jehovah explained to the Israelites His intent for their lives. Of all the people of the earth He had singled out one nation, not simply for privilege, but for a task.

You shall be for me a kingdom of priests and a holy nation (Exod. 19:6).

Out of gratitude for their redemption, God expected Israel to display His glory in their lives. They were to be a nation that performed God's will on earth as it was done in heaven. As royal priests they had the dual responsibility of representing men to God and God to men. They were Jehovah's treasured possession — His holy people.

Keeping covenant was the means by which Israel could display to the world her creator. As the covenant begins, God identifies Himself, and then proceeds to state the reason why Israel should freely choose to enter this agreement (Exod. 20:2).

Identification: I am the LORD your God[3]
Explanation: I brought you out of Egypt
I brought you out of Slavery

The stipulations of this covenant are called the ten commandments. Compliance to these commands was a reasonable response especially in light of their redemption. As Redeemer, Jehovah expected their complete loyalty and devotion. He expected obedience to issue forth from a heart bubbling over with gratitude. Substitute deities were not to occupy the place of primacy that belonged to God and God alone. He had already demonstrated His dependability. He alone had liberated them and, therefore, He alone deserved their ardent worship.

HOW QUICKLY WE FORGET

"We will do everything the LORD has said; we will obey" (Exod. 24:7).With these words the children of Israel consented to bind themselves to the terms of the covenant. Moses then left camp and scaled Mount Sinai to receive from the Lord the tablets of stone. Excitement ran high. Anticipation was at a fever's pitch.

But the days passed on into weeks and weeks into a month. Moses, their visible representative of God, failed to return. Fear and anxiety increased. Something had to be done. Unrest spread through the camp like a wild fire.

It was decided that a visible symbol was needed to rally and unite the people. After all, it's infinitely easier to walk after the visible than it is to trust in the invisible (II Cor. 5:7). So an idol in the shape of a calf was constructed and the following day declared to be a festival to the Lord. Now remember of whom it is we are speaking. The very people who had first-hand experience of God's redemption, guidance, protection, and provision now become idol builders — just forty days after Moses left camp.

The Lord's anger blazed into an inferno as a result of their rebellion. Three thousand were immediately put to death by the sword as ordered by Jehovah. Since God's people refused to practice righteousness motivated by grace and gratitude, God resorted to punishment. What else could He do?

This principle is threaded throughout scripture. Nadab

and Abihu failed to sanctify God in their hearts so the Lord showed Himself holy in the eyes of all Israel through judgment upon them (Lev. 10:1-3). Isaiah declared that when God's judgments come upon the earth, the people learn righteousness (Isa. 26:9). See also Ezekiel 28:22 and Amos 3:2. We must never forget that if we fail to acknowledge God's holiness willingly, then a forced acknowledgment of His holiness will come through judgment.

REJECTION AND REPLACEMENT

Jehovah, who so recently redeemed them, was summarily replaced by a lifeless idol of their own making. The new covenant, so recently established, was also rejected. Moses clearly understood the implications of their idolatrous conduct. He graphically demonstrated what they had done by breaking God's stone tablets in full view of the people (Exod. 32:19). From that moment onward a cloud of deep despair and regret enveloped the camp of Israel.

However, God was still gracious. That rebellious generation would eventually die off in the wilderness. Thirty-eight years after Kadish Barnea the old patriarch Moses addressed a new generation. The majority of those who were present at Sinai and remembered what had transpired there were already dead and gone. Moses, the wise grandfather, tenderly reviewed the law a second time for his 'grand-children' who were about to take possession of the promised land. Deuteronomy (meaning the second law or repeated law) contains the sermons Moses proclaimed to this new generation while camped east of the Jordan.

His message was short and concise. Whole-hearted obedience to the Lord is indispensable. He instructed them that

17

the land they were about to receive was a gift from their God. Furthermore, he reminded them that the keeping of the land was inextricably connected to their keeping of the convenant. The covenant itself contained sanctions for disobedience and blessings for obedience enumerated in Deuteronomy 28-30. The land's previous inhabitants had defiled it through their abominations. Now Israel was to purify the land through practical holiness (Lev. 18:24-30).

Aware of the potential danger, this series of sermons is punctuated with numerous commands and prohibitions concerning idolatry:

> Don't make idols — 4:15-30
> Decalogue restated — 5:8
> Don't follow foreign Gods — 6:14; 7:16,25f; 8:19; 11:16
> Debacle with the Golden Calf — 9:17-21
> Demolish foreign altars — 12:1-3,29-31
> Destroy false prophets — 13:1-11
> Don't assimilate idols into your worship — 16:21f

In fact the first curse to be pronounced from Mount Ebal after they crossed the Jordan was,

> Cursed is the one who makes any carved or molded image, an abomination to the LORD, the work of the hand of the craftsman, and sets it up in secret (Deut. 27:15).

The people would give their assent by shouting "Amen" — so be it.

This revival meeting east of the Jordan lasted approximately one month. As the time ticked away Moses knew his death was near. So he assembled the nation one last time and in their hearing, recited Israel's history in the form of a song. In that recitation idolatry was given a considerable amount of attention.

18

Jeshurun grew fat and kicked; you grew fat, you grew thick, you are covered with fat; then he forsook God who made him and scornfully esteemed the Rock of his Salvation. They provoked him to jealousy with foreign gods; with abominations they provoked him to anger. They sacrificed to demons, not to God . . . Of the Rock who begot you, you are unmindful, and have forgotten the God who fathered you. They have provoked me to jealousy by what is not God; they have moved me to anger by their foolish idols. (Deut. 32:15-17a, 18, 21).

More will be said later of Paul's use of this passage in the Corinthian letter. The crucial issue for you to understand at this point is that idolatry is tantamount to . . .

Abandoning God
Rejecting the Savior
Deserting the Rock
Forgetting God

WHAT'S VALUABLE TO YOU

Not only is idolatry a rejection of the true God; it's also the worship of a false god. Martin Luther defined a god as "That upon which your soul relies and in which your heart delights." In other words, idolatry is trusting in something or someone other than God for happiness and/or security. Therefore, idolatry can be viewed as a sin of commission — that is, we willingly place our trust in a wrong object or person. Idolatry can also be viewed as a sin of omission — that is, we fail to give God the honor He's entitled to. Perhaps Tertullian was right in his assessment that idolatry is the "whole procuring cause of judgment" upon the earth.

Consider some personal questions as a means of application. Who or what at this moment is the most important thing in the world to you? Who or what do you think about time and time again when your mind isn't engaged with your occupation or with someone else?

Keith Miller helps us understand this concept by using the analogy of a cheap dime store toy: a paddle ball. The rubber ball is attached to the wooden paddle by a long thin piece of elastic. When the ball is struck by the paddle it will fly only as far as the elastic allows. Then the ball is snapped back to the paddle and the process is repeated.

Who or what consistently returns to your mind over and over again as the tensions of life subside? Is that dominant thought Jesus? If not, perhaps you've got a problem with idolatry. You've already seen that God demanded Israel's primary love. Jesus also demands our primary love. Both refuse to settle for second place. The reason for their demand will be explained in the next chapter.

Because of the freedom Jehovah obtained for Israel, He expected them to have "no other gods before me." Because of the freedom Jesus, our Passover Lamb, has purchased for us, He demands that His disciples have no other gods before Him. If you love anything or anyone more than you love Jesus, then you cannot be His disciple. Sound demanding? Well, I didn't say it; God incarnate did. "So likewise whoever of you does not forsake all that he has cannot be my disciple" (Luke 14:33). As Augustine alertly observed, "Christ is not valued at all unless he is valued above all."

Hopefully you're beginning to see that according to God, idolatry has far greater ramifications than the narrow, restrictive limits offered by our Western culture. Would you now agree with the assertion that we have a problem in our culture with idolatry? Hopefully the remaining chapters will help you to identify some idols that may presently reside in your heart and, once identified, it's my prayer that God's grace will motivate you to smash these hindrances to holiness in order that God may use you in a powerful way.

Questions for Discussion

1. Define idolatry.
2. Explain how idolatry is fraud.
3. What is the dual responsibility of priests? Since all Christians are priests, describe how we fulfill each task today.
4. What is the "reasonable response" which God expects from the redeemed?
5. Why are there numerous warnings concerning idolatry in the book of Deuteronomy?
6. Discuss the statement "Christ is not valued at all unless He is valued above all."
7. Would you agree that we have a problem in our culture with idols? If so, name a few.

Endnotes

1. Tertullian, *On Idolatry*, Chapter 1.
2. Colin Brown, *Dictionary of New Testament Theology*, vol. 2, (Grand Rapids: Zondervan Publishing House, 1976), p. 284.
3. God identifies Himself by the divine name YHWH normally pronounced YAHWEH, (Exod. 3:14, 6:4). It means, I am who I am, or, I will be what I will be; indicating that He alone is the self-existent one, totally free from the control of others.

be careful in choosing your god

In the last chapter we learned that idolatry is trusting in something or someone other than God for happiness and security. Hopefully, you were impressed with the fact that God absolutely refuses to play second fiddle to anyone or anything.

The question that now lies before us is, Why? Why does God demand such commitment on our part? Why does He prohibit the worship of other gods? Is this the demand of a tyrant? Is it just? Why is it imperative that we love God with all our heart, soul, mind and strength (Deut. 6:5; Mark 12:13)?

The answer to our 'Why' question can be summarized in one sentence. A person comes to be like his God, regardless of who or what that god may be. In this chapter we'll consider this principle.

GOD'S INTEREST: OUR WELL-BEING

God has chosen to reveal His will to us for our own

benefit; for our physical and spiritual well-being.

I am the LORD your God who teaches you what is *best for you*, who directs you in the way you should go (Isa. 48:17, NIV; italics mine).

In order for holiness to become a reality in your life, you must be completely convinced of this fundamental truth. God's laws have been made known for your benefit. His ways are always superior to ours.

God the creator and designer of the human race is well aware of what is best for man and society. If Israel had only been convinced that God's law was for their optimum benefit, then they would not have rejected Him for worthless idols.

If Israel, or any society for that matter, conscientiously chose to obey the Ten Commandments would that not constitute a safe and strong society? Of course it would. God knew that society would function harmoniously if murder, adultery, theft, lies, and covetousness were absent. He knew that man's chief happiness could be obtained if he had no other gods before Him.

Every parent understands the difference between rules designed for their children's well-being and rules designed for the parents' benefit. "Go outside and play" or "Go upstairs and be quiet" usually are not said with the children's welfare in mind. Normally they're said because your child is disturbing you or interrupting your concentration. "Don't play in the street"; "Don't lean out the window" are rules of an altogether different sort.

God's laws are like the latter. Spiritually, physically and emotionally, He has our welfare in mind. A surgeon once remarked to E. Stanley Jones, "I've discovered the kingdom of God at the end of my scalpel. It's in the tissues. The right thing morally is always the healthy thing physically."[1] Many of the social diseases which presently plague our country stem directly from an abandonment of God's moral principles. Societies always function best when God's will is respected and obeyed. An examination of the history of the human race would seem to suggest that the outcomes have been better when men lived on the assumption of the existence of God than when they assumed the opposite.[2]

Moses viewed God's revealed will as beneficial and not burdensome.

For it is not a futile thing for you, because it is your life (Deut. 32:47).

So did David:

The Law of the Lord is perfect, converting the soul . . . making wise the simple . . . rejoicing the heart . . . enlightening to the eyes . . . in keeping them there is great reward (Psa. 19:7-11).

And Jesus:

My yoke is easy and my burden light . . . I have come that they may have life, and that they may have it more abundantly (Matt. 11:30; John 10:10).

And John:

For this is the love of God, that we keep his commandments. And his commandments are not burdensome (I John 5:3).

God has more than adequately proven His love for us. Therefore, we can trust His word without fail. He has our best interests at heart when He demands our primary and unqualified love. We're not in a position to modify or minimize the Lord's message in this matter. We don't ap-

proach the Bible in order to judge its worthiness or accep-
tability; on the contrary; it judges us (Heb. 4:12). You rob
potential, power, and peace of mind from yourself every
time you ignore God's directives and give your devotion to
another.

The story is told of the "gentleman thief," who was Arthur Barry. He was the quintessential jewel thief of the
roaring-twenties. Eventually, after a long crime spree, a
jealous woman turned him in to the police. He spent the
next eighteen years in prison.

Upon his release he settled in a small New England
village and lived a modest life. Word soon leaked out,
however, concerning his identity. Reporters flocked to his
residence to interview this famous criminal.

One day a young probing reporter asked, "Mr. Barry,
you stole from a lot of wealthy people during your years as a
thief. Do you remember the one from whom you stole the
most?"

"That's easy," Barry replied, "The man from whom I
stole the most was Arthur Barry. I could have been a successful businessman, a contributing member of society, but
instead I chose a life of crime and spent two-thirds of my
adult life behind bars."

So it is when you choose to ignore God's revelation.
You end up hurting yourself.

GOD'S INTENT: REFLECTION

As the moon reflects the glory of the sun; the children of
God are to reflect the glory of their Creator. Our Father isn't
satisfied with our petty self-righteousness. He wants His
people to reflect His righteousness. We're His royal am-

bassadors, His kingdom of priests (Exod. 19:6; I Pet. 2:9). Redemption is the theme of the book of Exodus, while the theme of the following book of Leviticus is sanctification. The theme of holiness runs throughout this book. The phrase 'holy unto Jehovah' is found 83 times in its 27 chapters. As a nation, Israel was to be holy because the God who redeemed them was holy (Lev. 11:45; 19:2; 20:7).

What is holiness? The Greek for holy, *hagios*, means that which is separated from the common. The antonym for holy is profane. To be holy implies the fact that one has been dedicated to God and/or the service of God. Israel spent almost a year at Mount Sinai learning from God what it meant to be a 'holy nation' (Exod. 19:1 to Num. 10:11). Holiness influenced not only their worship, but it had personal, family, and social implications as well (Lev. 17-20). As long as the nation kept itself free from idolatry and practiced holiness, it was a light for the Gentiles; reflecting the glory of God. However, when they failed, God brought swift retribution because His holy name was being profaned among the nations (Isa. 52:5; Ezek. 36:22; Rom. 2:24).

Israel was designed to showcase God's glory. The church of Christ today is called to the same task.

> But as he who called you is holy, you also be holy in all your conduct, because it is written, "Be holy, for I am holy" (I Pet. 1:15f).
> But you are a chosen generation, a royal priesthood, a holy nation, his own special people, *that you may proclaim the praises of him*, who called you out of darkness into his marvelous light (I Pet. 2:9).

Notice that in the first quotation Peter makes reference to the book of Leviticus. The principle of holiness, and all its implications, is still applicable for the church today. Second:

note God's purpose for making us a holy nation: "that you may proclaim" His praises! This phrase is an intensified form of the word *anangello*, which means to announce or report. In this text it means to proclaim aloud by word or action.

So how's your proclamation? Perhaps you've set apart some idol on the throne of your heart and, therefore, you're unable to adequately reflect God's glory in your life. If so, that idol must be dethroned. After all, we're presently the only light this dark world has, and our Father wants His glory reflected. Reflected to the extent that unbelievers will see your good deeds (I Pet. 2:12) and be impelled to ask you about the faith they see demonstrated in your life (I Pet. 3:15).

GOD'S IDEAL: TRANSFORMATION

The third reason that God prohibited idolatry is because man is created in such a way that he is destined to become like that which he worships. This is the reason Jehovah desires our total heartfelt worship. Your best interests, and mine, lie at the heart of the prohibition against idols.

We're now considering one of the greatest truths contained in scripture: the honor and privilege of being transformed into the likeness of the King of the Universe.

The Psalmist discusses the idolatry of the surrounding nations in Psalm 115. He declares in verse 8 that,

> Those who make them are like them; so is everyone who trusts in them.

This inspired writer assures us that the worshipper will become like that which he worships. The Creator has woven this law into the very fabric of the universe in which we live. Much later in Judah's history, the prophet Jeremiah would weep and lament over his kinsmen's idolatry. The Lord instructed Jeremiah to proclaim the following message in the hearing of the people of Jerusalem.

What fault did your fathers find in me, that they strayed so far from me? They followed *worthless idols* and became *worthless themselves* (Jer. 2:5, NIV; italics mine).

In the foreword to his book *Campus Gods on Trial*, Chald Walsh rightly remarked,

The god or God that you select will go to work and remake you in His image. After serving your particular deity for twenty years, you will be a very different person . . . (just as ideas have consequences) . . . Gods have still greater and more permanent consequences — in you.[3]

If money is your god then your life will become as unstable and insecure as the dollar. If popularity is your god, you'll lose your own identity and begin to seek identity from the crowd. If pleasure is your god then life will become shallow and superficial. Life will become a never-ending journey of hopping from one thrill to the next. If lust is the object of your worship, then you'll end up cheapened and degraded. I could go on and on, but I think you see the point. "The difference in men is not in their talents, but in their dedications," observed writer Ralph Waldo Emerson. The object of your dedication will invariably determine the outcome of your life. By giving God the glory and honor He so rightly deserves, you guarantee for yourself a glorious and personal transformation into His image (Rom. 8:29).

The Scripture often speaks of Jehovah as a jealous God (Exod. 20:6; Deut. 31:16; I Cor. 10:22; I Cor. 11:2). The

Lord's jealousy is His zeal to protect someone supremely precious to Him. It's the zeal we feel when an intruder threatens the relationship we have with our spouse or children. We want our loved one protected. We diligently seek their highest good. God in like fashion jealously longs for our full devotion, because He alone *is* our highest good. When He has our hearts the transformation will commence.

The apostle Paul has much to say about this wondrous transformation process in II Corinthians 3. He does so by drawing a contrast between Moses and the present ministers of the new covenant. Under the old covenant only one man experienced this glorious transformation — Moses. The details are recorded in Exodus 33-34. Through standing in God's presence, Moses was gloriously transformed (II Cor. 3:8). However, that glory slowly faded away (II Cor. 3:18). He lacked an inner dynamic to continually radiate God's glory in his life.

That dynamic is now provided for those in the new covenant. That dynamic is God's indwelling Spirit!

> And we who with unveiled faces all reflect the Lord's glory are being transformed into his likeness with ever-increasing glory, which comes from the Lord, who is the Spirit (II Cor. 3:18, NIV).

What a powerful passage! Under the old covenant only one man reflected the Lord's glory, while under the new covenant all men and women, boys and girls, can reflect the Lord's glory. Praise God! What a privilege!

Again we come face to face with the truth we've been discussing: the object of your worship determines the outcome of your soul. A man becomes like his God. Notice, however, that this transformation is not one-sided. It requires mutual participation between the human and Divine.

We can, and do, play a part in creating the proper conditions in which this growth can take place.

Your Part:
1. Get unveiled. Refuse to cover up any area of your life to the Lord. Stop rationalizing your sins and shortcomings. Develop an honest, submissive, and sincere spirit. Learn to let the piercing light of God's word shine into every dark crevice of your soul.
2. Reflect or meditate upon God's glory. In other words, saturate your mind with Jesus. He alone perfectly declared the Father's glory. Focus your faith on Him. Let Christ be the dominant thought that constantly returns to your mind over and over again throughout the course of the day (II Cor. 4:6; John 1:18; 14:9).

God's Part:
3. He works the miracle of transformation. That's a promise. God's Spirit is the agent of this transformation. You are merely the object of transformation. Refuse to extinguish His holy fire and you will experience ever progressive and permanent transformation into the Lord's likeness.

This transformation is not something we pull off on our own. It's not anything that we can take credit for or boast about. Rather it's a change which occurs from the inside out. C.S. Lewis accurately observed that Christianity is not,

> reading the words of Christ and trying to carry them out in our lives, as a person would read Plato, Ghandi, or Marx and try to carry them out. Christianity says that a real person, Jesus, is living in you and doing things to you, transforming you, recreating you into a son of God like himself![4]

There's the dynamic — the power. The son of God became man so that men could become sons of God (John 1:12; II Cor. 5:21). I don't have to act as *if* He is with me, He *is* with me in the person of His Holy Spirit.

31

J.B. Philips described the personal presence of the Spirit with this simple example. If you're writing a poem and the rhymes won't come or the lines won't fit you may cry, "Oh, William Shakespeare, help me!" and nothing whatever happens. If you're feeling jittery you may think of some hero of the past like Nelson, and say, "Oh, Horatio Nelson, help me!" But again there isn't the slightest response. But if you're trying to lead a Christian life and realize you're coming to the end of your own moral strength and you cry, "Oh, Christ, help me!" something does happen. There is a living Spirit immediately available, and millions have proved his existence.[5]

If you hunger for such a transformation, then fill your mind with Jesus. Put no other gods before Him and enthrone Him as the sole object of your worship and devotion. Transformation will then begin.[6]

CONCLUSION

In order for God's intent and ideal to be realized in our lives, we must purposefully fix our thoughts and eyes on Jesus (Heb. 3:1, 12:2).

Several years ago while in college, I met a young man who was raised in the restoration movement. His mother, a Christian, faithfully took him to church as he grew up. He heard the Bible lessons and he learned the right theology. When I met him, he was doing his undergraduate work in religious studies in order to enter the seminary — to become a rabbi in reformed Judaism.

One day I asked him if he could tell me what had happened to change his way of thinking.

He paused for a moment and then replied, "I guess I

never had Jesus as the center of my life." His answer is so relevant to our discussion. Every disciple needs to look into his heart and ask, "Do I have Jesus as the center of my life?" If not, then we've cheated ourselves and have dishonored our Lord who died in order that we might live.

Questions for Discussion

1. Why must we be careful in choosing our God?
2. What fundamental truth concerning God's revelation must we firmly believe in order to be holy? Explain your answer.
3. Do you feel most Christians see God's commands as beneficial or burdensome? Explain your answer.
4. Define holiness.
5. How would you explain the jealousy of God?
6. What two things are necessary on our part in order to be transformed?
7. Who is the agent of transformation?
8. Does the realization that we can't transform ourselves but that God can, encourage you? Explain your answer.

Endnotes

1. E. Stanley Jones, *The Divine Yes*, (Nashville: Abingdon Press, 1975), p. 51.
2. Source unknown.
3. Chad Walsh, *Campus Gods on Trial*, (New York: MacMillan Publishing Co., 1953), p. XIV.
4. C.S. Lewis, *Mere Christianity*, (New York: MacMillan Publishing Co., 1952), p. 164.
5. J.B. Phillips, *Plain Christianity*, (London: Epworth Press, 1960), pp. 101-102.

6. I'm assuming that you've already complied with the terms required of you by our Lord Jesus in order to receive the indwelling of his Holy Spirit (John 3:3-5; Acts 2:38, 5:32; I Cor. 12:13; Gal. 3:26f, 4:6; John 7:38f).

3

idolatry: a nagging problem

It's a well-worn truism known by many, and because it's so familiar, it often loses its punch. Familiarity, however, does not discredit or negate the truth of the saying. Centuries upon centuries of careful observation have proven it valid — time upon time again. The statement? Those who fail to learn from history are destined to repeat its mistakes.

The prophets of old would whole-heartedly concur. So would the apostles. They both labored among a people who, like their forefathers, failed to learn from the mistakes of the past and constantly resisted the Holy Spirit (Acts 7:51f).

We will briefly look at the efforts of three men of God, who pled with their people to forsake their man-made gods and return to the God who made man. These men were Isaiah, Jeremiah, and Paul.

ISAIAH

The Call

The Lord God called Isaiah to prophetic service in the year 740 B.C. While in the temple, Isaiah had a vision of the heavenly king. He experienced the glory and holiness of the Lord Almighty (Isa. 6). The prophet recorded the precise time at which this vision occurred, "In the year King Uzziah died, I saw the Lord."

That date is important. Uzziah was the most powerful Judean king to follow Solomon. During his fifty-two year reign, Judah flourished like a choice vineyard. Perhaps despair concerning the nation's future had driven Isaiah to the temple to pray. The earthly powerful king in whom they trusted was now dead. In his place his son, Jotham, had taken the throne. Rumors of war abounded. The nation was sick, scared, and trembling. And like Israel at Sinai without Moses, Judah would eventually look for help in all the wrong places.

The Confrontation

At this point it would be helpful for you to open your Bible and familiarize yourself with the historical background of Isaiah 7 recorded in II Kings 15:32 — 16:20 and II Chronicles 27-28. Jotham was a good king like his father, but neither he nor Uzziah destroyed the high places. The taint of idolatry, therefore, remained in Jerusalem.

Ahaz, on the contrary, enthusiastically embraced idolatry; including human sacrifices! The physical idols were merely an outward expression of the king's lack of trust in

36

Jehovah's ability to meet his needs. And his needs at that time were many.

Israel and Aram (Syria) had joined forces in order to stand against their common enemy, Assyria. They wanted Ahaz of Judah to join this political alliance. When Ahaz refused, they marched on Jerusalem and Ahaz lost 120,000 in one day. Panic prevailed (v. 2). At the same time, the Philistines were causing trouble in the southern portion of Judah. Ahaz found himself helplessly trapped in the middle (734 B.C.).

At this point the Lord instructed Isaiah to go and confront Ahaz (v. 3). The present terrors being poured out on Judah were the work of God's divine discipline. He wanted the nation to turn from their idols and once again trust in His power. Isaiah offered a message of hope for the kingdom, but Ahaz was convinced that the situation was far too big and complex for God to handle.

Isaiah's word to Ahaz was clear: God is with us!

Do not be afraid of their threats, nor be troubled. The Lord of hosts, him you shall hallow; Let him be your fear, and let him be your dread. He will be as a sanctuary (Isa. 8:12f).

Quite a message considering the circumstances. But Ahaz didn't look to God for his security. Instead he paid tribute to Assyria and enlisted their help. He preferred to trust in visible military might rather than in the Lord of hosts. Of course Assyria was more than willing to oblige. In 732 B.C. Syria fell and in 721 B.C., after a three year siege the ten northern tribes were destroyed and carried into Assyrian captivity But God wasn't finished with the "rod of his anger" (Isa. 10:5-19).

When Hezekiah, the son of Ahaz, came to the throne the spiritual condition of Judah improved. Under Isaiah's influence, he dismantled the high places and destroyed the idols of worship. He ultimately refused to pay tribute to Assyria and declared independence from them.

In a stormy rage Assyria moved against Judah. Forty-six fortified cities of Judah fell to Sennacherib's advancing armies. Only Jerusalem remained — surrounded — shut up "like a bird in a cage" (701 B.C.).

Isaiah's message to his king was once again, "do not be afraid"; "Put your trust in the Lord" (Isa. 37:6). This time Isaiah's advice was taken and Hezekiah went up to the temple to pray (Isa. 37:14-20). That night an angel of the Lord descended and put to death 185,000 Assyrians (Isa. 37:36). God intervened, not because of Judah's faithfulness, but because His reputation was on the line.

Application

The apostles Paul and Peter applied the spiritual truth of Isaiah 8 to the Christians of their day (Phil. 1:28; I Pet. 3:14f). The church is not to fear the things that the world does: war, inflation, depression, death, etc. . . . We are called not to put our trust and hope for security in strong leaders, military might or even bank accounts. We must learn to trust the Lord and obey Him in spite of the circumstances. True faith doesn't minimize the difficulties, but it does magnify God! It persistently obeys even in the midst of perplexities (II Cor. 4:7-10).

JEREMIAH

The Call

Seventy-four years after the Lord saved Jerusalem from

the Assyrians, another prophet was summoned into action — Jeremiah. Jeremiah's career would span a period of forty-one years, a career that would witness the destruction of the temple and Jerusalem: the city he loved. God assured this young prophet that he was the right man for the job. His message wouldn't be pleasant nor easy, but it was God's message and so it had to be spoken. Jehovah promised His novice prophet, "I am with you to deliver you" (Jer. 1:8).

His World

Five years after Jeremiah's call, King Josiah initiated religious reform in Jerusalem, calling people back to the book; removing from the temple the idols of Baal and Asherah (II Kings 22-23). He did away with the pagan priests and desecrated the valley of Hinnom. His reform, however, was too little, and too late. His external reforms failed to reform the hearts of God's people.

Mighty Assyria fell to the Babylonians in 612 B.C. Babylon, as prophesied by Isaiah, then set her bloodthirsty sights on Judah. Jeremiah's task was to inform his own people, "Jerusalem will fall as a result of forsaking Jehovah and worshipping gods their hands had made" (Jer. 1:13-19).

The Reaction

Instead of humbling their hearts in repentance, the people and priests discredited Jeremiah's message. While Jeremiah faithfully preached "repent or perish" the priests salved everyone's consciences by saying "Peace, peace, everything's just fine. Don't take this fanatic Jeremiah too seriously." (6:13-15,8:11f).

The priests and people said this because their trust had been placed in two objects other than God. First, they looked to Egypt for aid and assistance against Babylon just as their fathers looked to Assyria under similar circumstances. Jeremiah warned them that they'd be sadly disappointed (Jer. 2:13-36). In 605 B.C. his warnings became reality. Egypt was crushed by the Babylonian forces at Carchemish. Egypt was now useless to them.

The second object of their trust was the temple. They considered the Holy City inviolable as long as the temple stood. God saved them in 701 B.C. under similar circumstances and they thought He'd surely do it again.

Jeremiah's famous 'temple sermon' is found in chapter 7. Jeremiah told the worshippers that they needed to reform their ways and their actions (v. 3). If the Lord's demands were met then they would live in the land. The proof of their sincere repentance would be,

1. Just dealing with each other, v. 5
2. Care for the alien, orphans and widows, v. 6
3. Refusal to shed innocent blood (human sacrifices), v. 6
4. Refusal to follow other gods, v. 6

However, instead of repentance, they trusted in ritual, and in the deceptive words of their priests. The result was that in 587 B.C. Nebuchadnezzar razed Jerusalem and the temple to the ground and carried the survivors off into captivity!

Application

It's so easy to put one's trust and find one's security in

right rituals. The vain philosophy that states that if the externals are practiced in the right place, in the right way, at the right time, then one is acceptable to God, is still with us in the church today. It is religion without repentance, external forms without internal realities. As the Jew trusted in his association with the temple, many Christians trust in their association with the Church of Christ.

The church at Laodicea possessed all the right externals, the right name above the door, the right type of church government; they practiced the right baptism, (i.e. immersion) they partook of the right emblems in the Lord's supper, and they assembled on the right day of the week. They did not, however, have Jesus in their hearts! (Rev. 3:20).

You mean it's possible to be scripturally immersed and not to have asked Christ into your heart? Jesus Himself said these brothers and sisters did just exactly that — and He should know!

I'm not indicating that externals are unimportant. Yet the Jews failed to hear Jeremiah's message of repentance because their trust was placed in their observance of the right external rituals. Centuries later they would miss the message of Messiah in the exact same way (Matt. 23:23f). Let's pray to God that we don't make the same mistake.

PAUL

No one made an impact upon the infant church as did Paul the apostle. We're first introduced to him at the stoning of Stephen, the first martyr for Christ (Acts 7:58). However, the persecutor would soon become the proclaimer. His conversion on the Damascus road was unthinkable by human standards. It was is if Hitler became a rabbi! Paul's conversion merely demonstrates the fact that no one it too far gone for our Lord Jesus to save (I Tim. 1:15f).

The Corinthians

Paul planted the church in Corinth during his second missionary journey (50-53 A.D.). Corinth was infamous as a seaport town infected with the vilest corruptions. Paul stayed on and instructed these new babes in Christ for a year and a half (Acts 18:11). They had a lot of maturing to do, a lot of habits to change. His first letter to them, written about 54 A.D., was a fatherly rebuke to his children for not living as they should under the Lordship of Jesus Christ (I Cor. 3:1-3; 4:14-16).

The Problem with Idols

Corinth had more than its share of pagan shrines and temples. The city, a vital seaport, was a melting pot for numerous cultures and religions. As such, idolatry was a problem with some of the new saints. Paul's discussion of this topic is found in I Corinthians chapters eight and ten. My purpose in this chapter is not to discuss the eating of meat sacrificed to idols, but rather to focus on what Paul had to say about the idols themselves.

His first point is that the idol itself is nothing (I Cor. 8:4; 10:19). The word idol means an unsubstantial form as we've already discussed in chapter one. There was no "God," no real existence in the heavens, which corresponded directly to the name of that idol. There never was a real existence, or God, by the name of Baal, Dagon, or anything else. The Bible does not teach polytheism but monotheism.

The second point concerning the idols is that even though the god worshipped is nonexistent, that worship does provide a means through which real demons can worm their way into the heart of the worshipper.

> Now am I implying that a false *god* really exists . . . Not at all! I say emphatically that the Gentile sacrifices *are made to evil spiritual powers* and not to God at all. I don't want you to have any fellowship with such powers (I Cor. 10:19f, Phillips translation; italics mine).

In this verse Paul refers back to Deuteronomy 32:17 where Moses, speaking of Israel, said "they sacrificed to demons, not to God." The distinction between God and demons must be kept clear. There is and always has been one God. There are, however, real created beings known as demons that do exist in our universe. These demons can influence the Christian while he is having fellowship with a nonexistent god.

I can see some of you smirking. You're thinking, "You aren't telling me that demons still exist are you?" Yes, I am. The same Jesus whom you trust for salvation believed in a real devil with real angels at his disposal (Matt. 25:41). On a number of occasions during His ministry He even cast out demons.

Paul reminded the Ephesian saints that their struggle, and ours, is not against flesh and blood but,

> against principalities, against powers, against the rulers of the darkness of this age, against spiritual hosts of wickedness in the heavenly places (Eph. 6:12).

Spiritual forces of evil still exist today. I may not fully comprehend the intricacies of the demonic hierarchy that Paul has just described, but nevertheless, I do believe in demonic forces just as much as I believe in angelic forces of light (Heb. 1:14).

There are two equal and opposite errors into which our race can fall about the devils. One is to disbelieve in their existence. The other is to believe, and to feel an unhealthy interest in them. They themselves are equally pleased by both errors and hail a materialist or a magician with the same delight.[1]

CONCLUSION

Will we repeat the mistakes of history? Will we fall prey to the same deceptions which victimized our spiritual forefathers? If we give our devotion to something or someone other than God, we have opened a door through which demonic influences can enter and warp our souls. It's not too late.

Seek the Lord while he may be found, call upon him while he is near. Let the wicked forsake his way, and the unrighteous man his thoughts; let him return to the LORD, and he will have mercy on him; and to our God, for he will abundantly pardon (Isa. 55:6,7).

Questions for Discussion

1. Discuss the timing of Isaiah's vision and call. What is the significance of seeing the Lord on His throne?
2. How do Peter and Paul apply the truth of Isaiah 8:12?
3. How can the church learn not to fear the things that nonchristians fear?

4. What were some of the religious reforms initiated by Josiah (II Kings 22-23)?
5. What message did the false prophets of Jeremiah's day proclaim?
6. Discuss in detail how the church of Christ can fall into the trap of trusting in rituals. Be specific.
7. Even though the god worshipped is nonexistent, what is the danger of idolatry? Explain your answer.
8. Are spiritual forces of evil still at work today? What scriptures support your answer?

Endnotes

1. C.S. Lewis, *The Screwtape Letters*, (New York: MacMillan Publishing Co., 1961), Preface.

the search for meaning

From the commencement of the covenant to the destruction of the temple some nine centuries later, the children of God have wrestled with idolatry. Since the beginning of the church in 30 A.D. idolatry has been a sin that has hindered the development of Christ-likeness in many believers. Are we so naive to come to the conclusion that we, in the twentieth century, have escaped idolatry's destructive influence?

IDOLATRY — A SPIRITUALIZED MEANING

The word of the Lord came to Ezekiel when some of the religious leaders of Israel came to speak with the prophet. God revealed to Ezekiel,

> Son of Man, these men have set up their *idols in their hearts* and put before them that which causes them to stumble into iniquity (Ezekiel 14:3, italics mine).

On two more occasions the phrase "set up idols in his heart" is used in this context (vv. 4,7). Idolatry, like all other activities of life, is the fruit of the overflow of the heart. Idolatry, therefore, begins in the heart.

Obviously, the Lord isn't speaking of some tangible, concrete, image erected inside of a man. Rather He's speaking of the spirit of idolatry which precedes the building of the physical idols. Since the beginning of their religious history, many of the leaders missed the spirit that lay behind the letter of the law. For instance, Jesus was not elevating the Law's demands in the sermon on the Mount. He enlightened the spirit of the law — something they had missed for centuries by looking only at the letter.

Paul spoke of covetousness as an act of idolatry! Clearly Paul has spiritualized idolatry in this verse. The covetous man or woman depends upon money or material possessions to bring happiness and security. They're not literally bowing down to a graven image, but their hope is in a false security. He instructed the Corinthians that the purpose of reading the recorded history of Israel is that they, (and we) might learn not to:

> lust after evil things as they also lusted. And do not become idolaters as were some of them (I Cor. 10:6f).

Idolatry can take many forms. Never assume that simply because you don't bow down to a graven image that idolatry can't be a personal problem. To assume such is to assume that since the outside of the cup is clean it necessarily follows that the inside of the cup is clean also. Such thinking is emphatically condemned by our Lord. The controlling inward passion of your life at this moment is your god. If that passion is not to please the Lord — then idolatry is a problem.

MAN — A STUBBORN SEEKER OF MEANING

Why do we turn to idols for security and happiness? Why, for that matter, do we turn to God for the same? The fact is, deep within the heart of each of us lies a yearning for meaning and fulfillment in life. Man is indeed "a stubborn seeker of meaning."

This wave of longing often sweeps over our hearts when we witness a gorgeous sunrise or a radiant sunset. It stirs within us as we marvel at the miracle of life as we hear the tender cries of a newborn baby. This strange emptiness invades our soul while we stand by the casket of a loved one, confronted with our own mortality.

No thinking person wants to feel that his life has been lived in vain. We want to feel as if our existence has bettered our world and those around us, be it ever so slightly. This universal desire gave birth to the inspirational film classic by Frank Capra: "It's a Wonderful Life."

A past head of the International Psychoanalytic Association of Europe discussed this nagging desire in the following way.

> Psychiatrists who are not superficial, have come to the conclusion that the vast neurotic misery of the world could be termed a neurosis of emptiness. Men cut themselves off from the root of their being, from God, and then life turns meaningless, goalless, empty — and sick. Then we get them.[1]

Victor Frankl, the eminent Jewish psychiatrist, wrote a book entitled *Man's Search for Meaning*. Frankl spent several years in the hellish Nazi concentration camps. His entire family perished in those camps, all but one sister. He, through firsthand observation of both guard and prisoner alike, concluded that the primary motivational force in one's life is a "will for meaning." A failure to find meaning and a sense of responsibility in one's existence, concluded Frankl, is the cause for man's neuroses. *"He who has a why to live for can bear almost any how."*

Dr. Norman L. Geisler, recognized by many as a leader in the field of apologetics, states,

> Every single human being worships something. Not everyone worships or believes in a god or gods in the same way, but everyone worships something. Even atheists worship something, whether that something is themselves, the universe or something else.[2]

This desire for meaning is a universal phenomenon unique only to man. If no real, genuine, fulfillment of this need can be found in life, then nature herself has played a cruel joke on us. We would experience the "ultimate cosmic alienation" — a spiritual quest to fill an unfillable void. Experience confirms the genuineness of this need. The question is: from where does this profound desire originate?

GOD THE SOURCE

The Bible contains a book that documents the explorations of one man's quest for meaning. The man was Solomon. The book is Ecclesiastes. Solomon was a man who had the time, the brains, and the money to conduct an extensive search. He experimented with education, sensual pleasures, architecture, art, wealth, and a host of other things searching for someone or something to calm the restlessness in his soul. He expressed the restlessness in these words.

> Meaningless! Meaningless! says the Teacher. Utterly meaningless! Everything is meaningless (Eccl. 1:2, NIV).

In his words you can feel his frustration with a purely secular existence. All of his attempts thus far to fill the void were nothing more than attempts to fit a square peg into a round hole. They just didn't work. Despair continued to reign. The ache remained unsoothed.

Frustration with life under the sun led him to look outside of this life to find meaning. He concluded that God was the one who had spoken his soul into existence (Eccl. 12:7). He further concluded that since God created the soul only He could satisfy its longings. No amount — no matter how great — of finite things could fill the infinite void. Only the Infinite could!

Ralph Waldo Emerson once wrote, "When God wants to carry a point with His children, He plants his arguments into the instincts." Man has an instinct for immortality, or in Solomon's words, "He has made everything beautiful in its time. Also He has put eternity in their hearts" (Eccl. 3:11).

God created us to be receptacles of Himself. There dwells in each of us a God-shaped vacuum at the center of our being. He intentionally made us with a piece of the puzzle missing so that dissatisfaction with this life would drive us to Him — the Source of satisfaction. In the opening paragraph of his *Confessions*, Augustine said,

> You made us for yourself and our hearts find no rest until they rest in you.

Good News. God, your Creator, wants to be found! He's not playing a galactic game of hide and seek with you. He has planted within your heart a restless yearning,

> so that they should seek the Lord, in the hope that they might grope for him and find him, though he is not far from each one of us; for in him we live and move and have our being (Acts 17:27f).

51

God wants to spend an eternity in fellowship with you. That is why He subjected the creation to frustration. If an ultimate fulfillment could be found in the things of this life, then we would lose our souls in the next life. It's an act of grace that put the desire for meaning in your soul. Countless thousands have, and now do, experience contentment, experience peace that passes all understanding in any and every situation, through the Christ who dwells in them. It's my prayer that you presently, or very soon will, experience His reality in your own life as well.

INADEQUATE RESPONSES

If you're unaware of the source of this restless longing then you're left to the methodology of trial and error as you relentlessly search for someone or something to validate your existence. Earlier we likened this desire to a vacuum. Nature abhors a vacuum. Remember the bell jars in high school science class? A vacuum is a depressurized space containing nothing. Yet it longs to draw whatever substance it can into that space to fill the void. The human spirit is just such a space within us that becomes a junk receptacle filled with whatever is nearest once the seal is broken.[3] Sex, drugs, alcohol, reputation, success, education, etc. . . . are sucked into vacuum in a feeble attempt to fill it. People look to these things for security and happiness. These things dominate their every waking thought, yet the restlessness continues to persist.

Others don't even attempt to fill the void. Instead they dilute, downplay, or in some cases even totally destroy the desire for meaning. This philosophy of life is called nihilism. Nihilism believes that human existence is absurd and meaningless. No ultimate reality exists.

Existentialism, a close second cousin, also asserts that the world is irrational but that man can insert truth and meaning into the universe. Yet there is no absolute truth but "one must instead find a truth which is true for him, an idea for which he can live or die." Truth becomes subjective, relative and situational; a concept presently held by millions of Americans.

Listen to the words of twentieth century philosopher Jean-Paul Sartre:

> The Existentialist finds it extremely embarrassing that God does not exist, for there disappears with him all possibility of finding values in an intelligible heaven . . . Everything is indeed permitted if God does not exist, and man is in consequence forlorn, for he cannot find anything to depend on within or without himself.[4]

and these words from atheist Bertrand Russell:

> The center of me is always and eternally a terrible pain — a curious wild pain — a searching for something beyond what the world holds . . . I do not find it, I do not think it is to be found, but the love of it is my life; it's like the passionate love for a ghost . . . ."[5]

These men have accepted the myth that nature has played a cruel joke on us humans. They believe that we live in a closed universe. For them no one stands outside. They, too, experience the "curious pain" but they fail to attribute it to the Creator. They merely leave it unfulfilled or block it out altogether. Either way, the result is a sad, lonely life upon earth; a life of quiet desperation.

CONCLUSION

Three truths are set forth in this chapter, which are

crucial for our understanding of idolatry.

1. God set eternity in our hearts so that we would seek Him as our chief happiness in life and eternity.
2. Some in their search for meaning are willing to settle for lesser gods: things or individuals that they look to for fulfillment, security, and happiness.
3. Trusting in something or someone other than God for security and happiness is a sin of the heart, the spirit of idolatry.

From this point on I'll devote the following chapters to the false gods of our time. Gods in whom many place their full trust and in whom some Christians place their partial trust; never fully denying the Lord, but also never fully accepting Him either.

Questions for Discussion

1. Where does the sin of idolatry begin?
2. Explain how covetousness is idolatry.
3. Discuss the statement "He who has a why to live for can bear almost any how." Do you agree? Are you speaking from personal experience? Share that experience with the class.
4. What do you think Solomon meant when he said "God has set eternity in the hearts of man"?
5. How does existentialism differ from nihilism?
6. Do you know people who are presently experiencing a void in their lives? How can you, as a Christian, help them fill it? Discuss your ideas.
7. What are some lesser gods that many in our society worship other than God?

Endnotes

1. E. Stanley Jones, *Victory Through Surrender*, (Nashville: Abingdon Press, 1966), p. 22.

2. Norman Geisler, *False Gods of Our Time*, (Eugene: Harvest House Publishers, 1985), p. 17.

3. Calvin Miler, *A Table of Inwardness*, (Downers Grove: Inter-Varsity Press, 1984), pp. 25-26.

4. Jean-Paul Sartre, taken from *No Wonder They Call Him Savior, by Max Lucado, (Multnomah Press, 1986), pp. 33-34.*

5. Bertrand Russell, taken from *Christianity Today*, (September 6, 1985): 25.

the god of self

In the first four chapters, we've witnessed a chronic tendency on the part of man to put his trust in false gods. We've also seen that there are real demonic forces presently at work in the world laboring to subvert our hearts and minds from the true God and to turn them toward lifeless idols. Some in our day look back upon Israel's history with stunned disbelief. Gods like Baal, Dagon, Ashtarte, Molech and others sound so antiquated and outdated. We wonder how the Israelites could have possibly served them instead of Jehovah.

Yet, today many Christians are playing the same song — second verse. The names of the gods have merely been changed to protect the guilty. Instead of those old fashioned gods of yesterday, many bow down to new gods with new names like Humanism, Scientism, Materialism, Hedonism, and Traditionalism; names which would sound extremely strange to those of Isaiah's day and age, but are all too familiar to us.

Our present age demonstrates a smug confidence about ourselves and our accomplishments. Many feel that we are at the pinnacle of a long upward trend and can, therefore, look down our noses at everything and everybody in the past.[1] This sort of chronological snobbery is totally unwarranted. Man himself has not changed much over the passing millennia. Nothing is ultimately new under the sun when it comes to the psychology of mankind or the temptations of the devil. The temptations which plagued Adam, Moses and David are the same temptations which plague us.

Thankfully, the scriptures provide us with a never-ending source of pertinent and practical information concerning who we are and how we think. "Everything that was written in the past was written to teach us," and, therefore, it's imperative to properly interpret these timeless truths and make the necessary applications to our day and age (Rom. 15:4).

THE DESIRE FOR AUTONOMY

Man was created to be the steward of God's world — a vice-regent to rule over the Lord's kingdom. Without a doubt man is a unique creation. He alone on this planet bears the image of his omnipotent Creator (Gen. 1:26f). Man is a finite being yet related to the infinite. Since this is so, he stands on the shores between time and eternity trying to determine which land will be his real home.

This indecision creates anxiety and insecurity, which is as God intended. This gnawing anxiety, however, offers an occasion for man to assert himself in an attempt to hide his insecurity and establish his own independence. Rather than building his house on the eternal, depending upon

God, he chooses to build his house on the temporal, depending upon himself. He desires to be autonomous — a law unto himself, making man (instead of God) the measure of all things. Pride and self-will provide the inspiration for this damning decision (Prov. 16:18).

MAN WAS NOT THE FIRST

Christianity and Dualism agree on one point — the universe is at war. The distinctiveness of the Christian message is that this war is not between two co-eternal, independent powers — one good, one evil. Instead, it's a civil war. A created subject intentionally rebelled in an attempt to depose the rightful king and steal his throne.

> And war broke out in heaven: Michael and his angels fought against the dragon; and the dragon and his angels fought, but they did not prevail, nor was a place found for them in heaven any longer. So the great dragon was cast out, that serpent of old, called the Devil and Satan, who deceives the whole world; he was cast to the earth, and his angels were cast out with him . . . And the dragon . . . went to make war with the rest of her offspring, who keep the commandments of God and have the testimony of Jesus Christ (Rev. 12:7-9,17).

One must be careful not to unduly literalize apocalyptic scripture. The style of apocalyptic scripture is highly metaphoric and symbolic. Yet, this scripture does contain a real, literal truth: Satan is at war with God and His church!

The honest student of scripture finds it difficult to be emphatically dogmatic about Satan and his fall as far as the details are concerned. Yet we do know that he fell, and the scriptures would seem to indicate that his fall came through pride. As John Milton aptly put it, Satan's philosophy was "Better to reign in Hell than serve in Heaven."[2] He was not willing to operate within his created role. He egotistically desired more.

Jesus referred to Satan's fall in Luke 10:18. Jude informs us that certain angels were not willing to submit to God's authority and were, therefore, cast into judgment (Jude 6). Peter refers to God's judgment upon angels who sinned (II Pet. 2:4). In his qualifications for elders, Paul comments upon the fact that conceit led to the Devil's fall (I Tim. 3:6).

The scripture which is often associated with Satan's demise is Isaiah 14:3-17. Similar language is found in Ezekiel 28:1-17. A careful reading will reveal that the primary subjects being discussed are the king of Babylon and the king of Tyre respectively. Yet the language is admittedly unique — even for apocalyptic scripture. Arrogance and pride are the motivating reasons for God's punishment upon both kings. But is it totally unthinkable that these heathen kings may be types of their demon Lord as David was of his Christ? Perhaps these earthly kings have followed the same prideful pattern as their spiritual counterpart and serve as shadows of his reality.

In any case, we do know that it was a stubborn refusal to submit to God's will which led to Satan's fall. This was the act of a traitor: one who contested altogether the sovereignty of his country and the right of his God to rule over him.[3] Such an act could not go unpunished. It's this rebellion that Satan is trying to seduce us into joining.

THE GARDEN

Pride is a form of self-deification. "Stubbornness is as iniquity and idolatry" (I Sam. 15:23). Inflated with our own egoism we erect the idol of our own will and bow down to it, rejecting the word of the Lord. We forsake our true glory and turn to our own way, trading the incorruptible for the corruptible.

What occurred in the garden of Eden is more than just mere history. It's a scenario that has been acted out by every mature adult since the beginning of time! It's the moment of time in which we reject a commandment-oriented life for one dominated and controlled by our own fleshly appetites. No longer will we live by what God has revealed. Instead we'll do as we feel and establish personal independence and autonomy.

In chapter three of Genesis, Satan cunningly comes in the form of a serpent. He who wanted to ascend to the throne has now descended into the form of a slimy snake. "Did God *really* say" — was enough to plant a seed of doubt in Eve's heart. "Perhaps I heard Him wrong," "Maybe I misinterpreted His meaning," were thoughts that possibly surfaced to her mind.

But she stood firm and responded to Satan's question.

> And the woman said to the serpent, "We may eat the fruit of the trees of the garden; but of the fruit of the tree which is in the midst of the garden, God has said, 'You shall not eat it, nor shall you touch it, lest you die' " (Gen. 3:2-3).

So now the Father of Lies altered God's word. The Lord said, "you shall surely die" but Satan responded, "you shall not surely die." He changed the command just a shade, merely enough to cast more darkness upon Eve's doubt. But instead of fleeing, she continued to reflect upon his lie.

Then the Devil began to appeal to her ego. He endeavored to make her believe that God was selfish and was withholding a better way of life from her by prohibiting the fruit of the tree. He persuaded her that she no longer had to function as a creature, but she could become like the Creator — she could be like God! (3:5). Since that day Satan has been peddling the same lie: the lie that we can obtain a better, more fulfilling life by doing our own thing, being our own master, rather than following the Lord's prescription for life.

The prodigal son swallowed this demonic lie hook, line, and sinker. This young, cocky kid was confident that he was in a better position to determine what was right for himself than his wise, experienced father. So he demanded his inheritance and split. Oh, it was fun for a while, but then he bottomed out. No friends. No money. No food. No source of income. Too stubborn to admit his mistake, he refused to go home. This young Jew began looking for a job and finally found one — slopping the hogs. Talk about adding insult to injury!

As a fifth-step counselor I've shared this story with many recovering alcoholics who have also become victims of the devil's lie. Many heard this parable for the very first time. Believe me, they can relate. It's always a joy to watch the glimmer of hope come to their eyes as I share the good news that the Father warmly accepted the prodigal back home. But first he had to "come to his senses" then take action and humbly return to his father confessing, "I have sinned against heaven and against you" (Luke 15:17-32).

Satan promised Eve that she'd be like God. Instead, she was cast out of the garden. The Devil promised the prodigal that good life. Instead, he found himself away from home destitute, downtrodden, and depressed. Two stories, thousands of years apart, but the temptation offered to both was identical — to ignore your Father's will, and do your own thing (Rom. 1:28).

GOD RESISTS THE PROUD

The book of Proverbs is a book of wisdom. Proverbs are condensed philosophies about life: moral, ethical and social snippets of inspired wisdom. Cervantes defined a proverb as, "A short sentence based on a long experience." They contain practical, down to earth instructions for daily living.

One truth is repeated throughout the book. God opposes the proud and detests all the proud of heart (3:34; 16:5). Some have reasonably argued that pride is the root sin from which all other sins sprout, grow, and bring forth their deadly fruit. The sin of pride is number one on the list of seven things that God hates (6:16). In one of the most quoted verses of Proverbs we learn that a haughty spirit precedes a fall (16:18). An interesting marginal notation is found alongside this verse in the Masoretic text. The notation reads, "the middle of the book." Isn't it interesting that the central truth of this great book about wisdom is that pride goes before destruction.

A few moments of meditation and reflection upon this truth will bring insight concerning why God hates pride. Pride doesn't like the idea of giving up one's will to God or to anyone else. Pride leads one to lean on his own understanding rather than seeking the Lord's will concerning a matter. Pride demands its own way regardless of the consequences.

The proud man refuses to admit his desperate need for the Lord. A man may be too big for God to use but never too small. Therefore, the first attitude necessary for true discipleship is that of being "poor in spirit." An individual who is "poor in spirit" is one who is totally dependent upon God, similar to a young child's dependence upon his father. Pride and "poor in spirit" are attitudes that stand one hundred and eighty degrees apart.

Kierkegaard once said, "God creates out of nothing — and everything which God is to use He first reduces to nothing." It's clear from scripture that God opposed the proud, but it's equally clear that God gives grace to the humble; a transforming and motivating grace for anyone who relies solely upon Him (James 4:6; I Cor. 15:10).

On the judgment day, when the entire human race stands before the throne of God there will be only two groups of people. Those who have said to God, "Thy will be done" and those to whom God says, "Thy will be done." All that enter the gates of Hell choose it.[5]

THE PHILOSOPHY OF ARROGANCE

Many Christians are deeply distressed at what they witness happening in our society; the breakdown of the family unit, the increase of crime, pornography and sexual permissiveness. Ethics seem to be gone with the wind. Parents have to instruct their kids about "good touch" and "bad touch." They must be extremely cautious, a caution that borders on paranoia, when going to the mall or allowing the kids to go outside and play. As unjust and terrible as these things are, they are merely the symptoms of a more serious disease — a cancer which is running rampant through the body of this nation.

The pop psychology of today sells millions of books telling us to Be Yourself, Find Yourself, Assert Yourself, Express Yourself and Satisfy Yourself. Narcissism fills the book shelves and the minds of many Americans. These superficial solutions, however, are not curing the ills of this sick society. The cause of the disease lies much deeper. A shift of values has taken place and a new value system has replaced the old.

A world view or value system is the way in which people look at themselves, their world, and the people around them. It defines their priorities. We may not be able to put a label on what our value system or philosophy of life is, but we possess and espouse one just the same whether we realize it or not.

One value system has set man on the altar of worship and makes man the center and measure of all things. This philosophical self-deification is called Humanism. Humanistic thought has influenced our educational institutions, media, and religious world. Christians are clearly not immune from its subtle influence.

Dr. Paul Kurtz, professor of Philosophy at New York State University and editor of the humanist magazine, *Free Inquiry*, has agreed that the following is a good definition of Humanism.[6]

> I use the word humanist to mean someone who believes that man is just as much a natural phenomenon as an animal or a plant; that his body and mind and soul were not supernaturally created but are products of evolution, and that he is not under the control or guidance of any supernatural being or beings but has to rely on himself and his own power.
>
> —Sir Julian Huxley

The American Humanist Organization has its own creedal statement called the Humanist Manifesto. The first Manifesto was drafted in Chicago in 1933 and signed by thirty-three men, most famous of whom was John Dewey, known as the "father of modern education." A second document was written in 1973. The signers of this document were also people of position and power: B.F. Skinner,

Professor of Psychology at Harvard; Norman Fleishman, executive Vice-President of Planned Parenthood World Population; Betty Freidan, founder of the National Organization for Women; and Alan Guttmacher, President of the Planned Parenthood Federation of America. These individuals obviously exercise a great influence over many segments of American society. Humanistic values have been introduced into our culture through such men and women.

In order to better understand the mindset of the humanist, consider the following presuppositions upon which their philosophy is built:

Religion:
First . . . We find insufficient evidence for belief in the existence of the supernatural . . . as non-theists we begin with humans not God, nature not deity . . . we can discover no divine purpose or providence for the human species . . . No deity will save us; we must save ourselves.

Second . . . science affirms that the human species is an emergence from natural evolutionary forces . . . There is no credible evidence that life survives the death of the body.

Ethics:
Third . . . Ethics are autonomous and situational needing no theological or idealogical sanction.

The Individual:
Sixth . . . In the area of sexuality, we believe that intolerant attitudes, often cultivated by orthodox religions and puritanical cultures, unduly repress sexual conduct. The right to birth control, abortion, and divorce should be recognized . . . . Short of harming others or compelling them to do likewise, individuals should be permitted to express their sexual proclivities and pursue their lifestyles as they desire.

The quotations are cited from the Humanist Manifesto II. A reading of these excerpts should be enough to convince any reader that New Testament Christianity and Humanism are diametrically opposed to one another. Humanists do not consider it worthwhile to retain the knowledge of God and, therefore, God has given them, and all who think like them, over to a depraved mind. The fruits of the depravity are flourishing in America today. Read Romans 1:28-31 and see for yourself.

APPLICATION

When you became a Christian you went out of the 'decision-making' business and went into the 'seeking the Lord's will' business. For the true disciple life is not simply doing what he or she pleases. Instead, it is prayerfully striving to choose what the Lord desires and act as the Lord would act in any given situation; realizing that each of us will give an account of himself to God (Rom. 14:7-12).

Christians must keep in mind that we're living in enemy-occupied territory. The challenge for us has always been to live in the world without allowing the world to live in us and the challenge was never greater. Our nation is reaping the harvest of years of influence from atheistic Humanism. Movies, videos, television, music, literature and the arts all show the influence of humanism. And, unless Christians exercise spiritual caution and selectivity in their participation in these activities, they too will be strongly influenced by secular thinking.

Consider the fact that adolescent suicide has increased three hundred percent from 1950 to 1980! We dare not close our eyes to such tragedies. These young people have been led to believe that life has no ultimate significance, value or purpose. They think of themselves as nothing more than 'dust in the wind.' Humanistic philosophy has deceived them about their true value and dignity in the sight of God, and about the purpose of their existence.

Pride is always a dangerous thing — especially religious pride. Jesus stands opposed to any form of religion that demonstrates a smug confidence in one's own righteousness and looks down spiritual noses at everyone else (Luke 18:9). The Laodiceans felt as if they'd arrived. They didn't need a thing. However, through heaven's eyes they were wretched, pitiful, poor, blind and naked (Rev. 3:17).

We must constantly guard against an arrogant, self-sufficient attitude. Consider how humanism may have influenced you the next time you're tempted to depend upon your own wisdom and understanding in handling a problem rather than humbling yourself in prayer and searching God's word for solutions (Prov. 3:5-7). We will never obtain the holiness God desires for our lives until we daily learn to submit through prayer, "Not my will — but Thy will be done," and be content to hear Him whisper, "Well done, my faithful servant." Armed with such a spirit, the idol of Humanism can and will be torn from our hearts.

Questions for Discussion

1. What does the phrase "chronological snobbery" mean? Is newer always better?
2. Define autonomy.
3. Why did Satan fall from heaven? Are there lessons here for us to learn? Explain your answer.
4. What do Genesis 3 and Luke 15 have in common?

5. Why does God hate pride?
6. Discuss the beliefs of the Humanist. Is it possible for Christians to be influenced by this way of thinking? Explain your answer.
7. What do you consider to be some of the reasons for the alarming increase in teenage suicide? How can we as parents make a difference?
8. How should Christian parents deal with their prodigal children? Be sure to read Luke 15:17-32 and discuss your ideas.

Endnotes

1. Kenneth E. Matthews, *C.S. Lewis and the Modern World*, Dissertation, University of California, Los Angeles, 1983, p. 54.

2. John Milton, *Paradise Lost*, (Book I, lines 262-263).

3. Selected Readings, *Faith in Search of Understanding*, (Nashville: Graded Press, 1968), No. 55.

4. Milton, op. cit., (Book 9, lines 168-169).

5. C.S. Lewis, *The Great Divorce*, (New York: MacMillan Publishing Co., 1946), p. 69.

6. Taken from the television transcripts of *The John Ankerberg Show*, (Chattanooga, "Secular Humanism"), Program 1, p. 1.

the god of peer approval

William James once said, "The deepest principle of human nature is the craving to be appreciated." The American psychologist Abraham Maslow is well known for his work concerning the hierarchy of human needs. Maslow believed that there are five basic needs that motivate all human beings. He ranked these needs in order of importance with number one being the greatest.

1. Physiological — the necessities of life such as food and drink
2. Protection — the preservation of life
3. Social needs — love and acceptance
4. Ego needs — recognition and status
5. Self Actualization — the purpose for one's life

According to Maslow, man will not show much concern for the lesser needs until the greater needs are satisfied. For instance, a man will show little concern for his ego needs if he's starving to death. Since many Americans have needs one and two fulfilled, the focus of our concern begins with number three. *We crave acceptance.* God has placed that need within our heart.

> The neighborhood bar is possibly the best counterfeit there is to the fellowship Christ wants to give His Church. It's an imitation dispensing liquor instead of grace, escape rather than reality, but it is a permissive, accepting, and inclusive fellowship. It is unshockable. It is democratic. You can tell people secrets and they usually don't tell others or even want to. The bar flourishes not because people are alcoholics, but because God has put into the human heart the desire to know and be known, to love and be loved, so many seek a counterfeit at the price of a few beers. With all my heart I believe that Christ wants His church to be . . . a fellowship where people can come in and say, "I'm sunk! I'm beat! I've had it!"[1]

It's imperative, therefore, to remind yourself of God's love and acceptance. If you don't, you may find yourself bowing to the idol of peer approval in order to fill that social need, and in so doing, compromise your faith.

No matter what you accomplish in life, God will never love you any more than He does right now. Our Father in heaven has no favorite children. He loves you just as much as the most eloquent evangelist or the most effective soul-winner. He loves the newest babe in the kingdom and the oldest soldier of the cross alike. You can't name one person past, present or future that Jesus died for more than for you. What a shot in the arm! What a boost to the ol' self-esteem! God thinks you and I are great!

CROWNED WITH GLORY AND HONOR

Self-esteem has been defined as the human hunger for the divine dignity that God intended to be our emotional birthright as children created in His image.[2] One result of the Fall was a perversion in the way man viewed himself. Fear and shame entered man's heart. Adam and Eve's self-image plummeted and they hid from God. Their sin cost them the divine dignity they once enjoyed.

The Bible portrays man as a unique creation. There is nothing on earth more like God than man.

> What is man that you are mindful of him . . . you made him a little lower than the angels, you crowned him with glory and honor, and set him over the works of your hands (Hebrews 2:6f).

Man's glory is that he is created in God's image. His honor is that God gave him dominion over the earth. This crown of dignity toppled from man's head when he sinned.

But God was still gracious. He replaced Adam and Eve's personal attempts to hide their shame with an acceptable covering. God made tunics of skin and clothed them (Gen. 3:21). Not only did God deal with their immediate guilt; He also promised the ultimate defeat of Satan (Gen. 3:15). It's clear that our Father doesn't want His children to swim in a pool of pity over past failures. A covering was and has been provided.

Why is a healthy, biblical self-esteem so important? It's important because God has designed individuals in such a way that you will consistently act according to the way you see yourself. Many criminals have a negative self-image. All their lives they've been told that they are "no good." Eventually they come to see themselves that way and act accordingly. The hatred they feel toward themselves and society finds expression through violent criminal acts. The final result is that often others tragically suffer from this man or woman's negative self-image. Parents, therefore, need to conscientiously work on helping their children construct a positive self-image that will see them through life.

GOD IS ON YOUR SIDE

God's love and acceptance can't be earned. It's already there. As mind-boggling as it may seem, that's what *Agape* love is all about. God has your best interest at heart. He is actively seeking your highest good no matter who you are and no matter what you've done.

God has provided the means through which our spiritual and emotional dignity can be restored. He has supplied a fountain through which we can be cleansed from fear and shame. Restored fellowship has been made possible. That which we were powerless to accomplish on our own, God did for us.

> But God demonstrates his own love toward us, in that while we were still sinners, Christ died for us. Much more then, having now been justified by his blood, we shall be saved from wrath through him (Rom. 5:8f).

God's love is powerful enough to save His enemies. Therefore, it's equally strong enough to save His friends. Christ's death was the means of our reconciliation while His life is the means of our preservation (v. 10).

Listen to the words of Jesus as He hung on the old rugged cross, "Father, forgive them, for they do not know what they do" (Luke 23:34). Christ offered this prayer for His persecutors. After man had done his worst — after they had subjected Jesus to public shame and humiliation — after inflicting enormous pain upon His body — Jesus still wanted them forgiven. In fact, Jesus was a soul-winner down to His dying breath. His promise of paradise to the penitent thief stands as an eternal testimony of God's willingness to forgive even the most undeserving of us.

Often you hear people say, "You don't know what I've done," or "How could God possibly forgive me," or "I'm not 'good enough' to be a Christian." You're absolutely right. You're not "good enough" to be a Christian and neither am I. But no one is beyond the Savior's prayer. It doesn't matter if you've shamed Him publicly or if you've humiliated His body. Jesus still wants you saved. God is on your side. It brings Him great pleasure to see people turn from their evil ways (Ezek. 33:11).

Paul reminds us in Romans chapter ten that you don't have to be super intelligent, super strong, or even super courageous to earn right standing with God. Provision has already been made. All you have to do is humbly choose to accept His provision, making Jesus the Lord of your life.

> But the righteousness of faith speaks in this way. "Do not say in your heart, 'Who will ascend into heaven?' (that is to bring Christ down from above) or, 'Who will descend into the abyss?' " (that is to bring Christ up from the dead). But what does it say? "The word is near you, even in your mouth and in your heart" . . . if you confess with your mouth the Lord Jesus and believe in your heart that God has raised him from the dead, you will be saved (Rom. 10:6-9).

In proving the point that we don't have to earn the right to hear God's word or enjoy God's fellowship, Paul quotes the words of Moses found in Deuteronomy 30. It's important to note the context of these words in order to feel their impact.

A new generation was about to cross the Jordan and inherit the land of promise. They clearly had not "earned" God's favor. For thirty-eight years they aimlessly wandered in the wilderness as a result of their rebellion. But God didn't destroy the nation. Once again He takes the initiative and sets before them "life and death, blessing and cursing." God brought His word near so that the Israelites might "choose life and live" (Deut. 30:19). Paul applies this to the work of Jesus. Christ has already left heaven and been raised from the dead, not because we're good, but because He's so good. So why not choose life and live?

Paul reminds the saints at Rome to receive or accept one another "just as Christ also received us" (Rom. 15:7). We all come to Jesus as sinners. God in His omniscience knows all about the skeletons in our closets. Yet if we are willing to come to Christ, He gladly receives us. We have our Lord's promise that whoever "comes to me I will by no means cast out" (John 6:37). No matter how well we dress or how "together" we appear to the world: the One who sees the heart knows that there is no saint without a past. The good news is that there's also no sinner without a future!

> If anyone is in Christ, he is a new creation; old things have passed away; behold, all things have become new (II Cor. 5:17).

Once these truths are grasped and internalized, a profound transformation of self-esteem takes place. Having come to Jesus on His terms, you realize that the most powerful, influential person in the Universe loves and accepts you. Once God has accepted you, it's no longer a matter of life or death for others to accept you. Now you're free to be who the Lord intended you to be, and the constant pressure to do and be what others expect diminishes. But if God's love and acceptance is not actualized in your life, then the acceptance and approval of others dominates your every action; and your personal uniqueness and freedom is sacrificed.

An old Norwegian folk tale tells of a boy who stumbled onto an egg lying at the base of a large tree. He gently picked up the egg, took it home; and placed it in a goose's nest. Days later the egg hatched. The creature that appeared looked nothing like the goslings. It's feet weren't webbed, but clawlike. It's beak was not flat, but pointed and twisted. Instead of lovely cream-colored down, this young bird was covered with ugly brown feathers. It didn't even sound like its friends in the barnyard. It tried, but never did fit in with the others.

One afternoon, weeks later, a giant eagle flew over the barnyard. The geese all ran for cover — all except the misfit. The young bird became excited when it saw the mighty eagle. Frantically, it began to flap its large wings until it left the ground and soared into the clouds. A startling discovery had been made. He had been trying to live like a goose, but was born an eagle.

God's acceptance should affect us in much the same way. It frees us to maximize our own unique talents and abilities that God has given to us. I don't have to be Abraham, Moses, or David. I don't even have to be Peter, James or John. All I have to be is to be fully me, and glorify the God of my fathers in all that I do.

THE PRAISE OF MEN VS. THE PRAISE OF GOD

John relates a sad story in the twelfth chapter of his gospel. There were rulers among the Jews who believed in Jesus as the Messiah, but refused to publicly confess their faith. Two explanations are given for their cowardly conduct.

1. They were afraid that they would be put out of the synagogue (v. 42.).
2. They loved the praise of men more than the praise of God (v. 43).

Before we become too critical of them, let me ask you a question. "Have you ever been in a restaurant and been ashamed or afraid to pray because of what others might think?" Here's a person sitting across from you who doesn't know you from Adam, and if the truth were known, couldn't care less if you lived or died. Jesus is also there. He's sufficiently proved His enormous love for you by dying for your sins. Have you ever been more concerned about what that stranger thinks, than about what Jesus thinks?

At times we are so foolish. We forget who truly cares.

I have this short prayer taped to the inside cover of my Bible, because I need a daily reminder of whose acceptance is truly important.

Lord, I renounce my desire for human praise, for the approval of my peers, the need for public recognition. I deliberately put these aside today, content to hear you whisper, "Well done, my faithful servant." Amen.

The need for social acceptance has caused believers to prostitute their principles and compromise their conduct. Such people need to allow the Holy Spirit to pour forth God's love into their hearts (Rom. 5:5). The brighter His love burns within my heart the drearier the acceptance of others becomes in comparison.

No one understood this like the apostle Paul. He at one time in his life was the least likely person in the world to be saved. But Jesus got a hold of his heart and things were never the same again. He wanted the world to know of the grace of God. He wanted others to experience redemptive freedom in Christ Jesus.

Paul, however, was not without his critics. He met opposition and obstacles time and time again as he ran the race God had marked out for him. Nevertheless, he discharged his duties as one "approved by God to be entrusted with the gospel" (I Thess. 2:4). Pleasing Christ, and not the world, was the indispensable goal of his ministry.

> . . . We speak, not as pleasing men, but God who tests the hearts . . . . Nor do we seek glory from men, either from you or from others, when we might have made demands as apostles of Christ (I Thess. 2:4,6).
> For do I now persuade men or God? Or do I seek to please men? For if I still pleased men, I would not be a servant of Christ (Gal. 1:10).
> Moreover, it is required in stewards that one be found faithful. But with me it is a very small thing that I should be judged by you or by any human court (I Cor. 4:2f).

Jesus is the same "yesterday and today and forever" (Heb. 13:8). While Jesus remains changeless the crowd is always changing. It's in a continual state of flux. That which is "in" today is "out" tomorrow. That which was fashionable yesterday may be repugnant today. Those who continually acquiesce and yield to popular opinion never know where they stand. They become a slave to the opinions of others. But those who are slaves of Christ know who they are and where they stand. Their lives are built upon the steadfast rock of ages and not the shifting sands of popular opinion.

According to an old Jewish fable, an elderly grandfather and his young grandson were taking their donkey to market. The grandfather led the donkey while the boy rode. As they passed through the first village, the villagers pointed and cried out, "How terrible! That young man has no respect for his elders!" So the boy changed places with his grandfather. He led while his grandpa rode the donkey.

As they passed through the next town, the people once again stared and pointed. They murmured, "How horrible. That old man is making that young boy walk in this heat." Upon hearing their remarks, they once again changed places. In the third village they were greeted as they were in the first. A new tactic was employed. Both decided to ride the donkey.

As they rode into the fourth village the people cried, "How inhumane. Look at that poor donkey!" When last seen leaving the village the lad and his grandfather were both walking — carrying the donkey.

CONCLUSION

In the world, and even in the church, it's obvious that we can't always please men with such discord. So why not determine to please the Lord. When you do, you'll find yourself accepted by all those who have adopted the same way of thinking.

Fear of peer disapproval and rejection has always been a snare. But the man or the woman who "trusts in the Lord shall be safe" (Prov. 29:25). God *is* on your side. He wants to unleash your own unique talents and abilities and free you from the pressure to conform to the will of others.

When we stand before God in judgment, all the applause and kudos of the world will be irrelevant. On that momentous day, you'll only be interested in the approval and acceptance of the one seated on the right hand of the Father. So why not daily seek the approval of Jesus and Jesus alone. If we all fixed our eyes on Jesus and practiced the following, our churches would once again be bubbling over with vitality and creativity.

I do the very best I know how, the very best I can, and I mean to keep on doing so until the very end. If the end brings me out all right, what is said against me will not amount to anything. If the end brings me out wrong, ten legions of angels swearing I was right would make no difference.

Abraham Lincoln

Questions and Answers

1. What are five basic needs that motivate all human beings?
2. Does God love the person who wins 100 people a year to Christ more than the person who wins one per year to Jesus? Explain your answer.
3. Define self-esteem.
4. Why is a biblical self-esteem important?
5. Discuss Jesus' prayer, "Father forgive them, for they do not know what they do." What is the significance of *when* Jesus offered this prayer? What is the significance of *why* He offered the prayer?
6. What point concerning salvation is Paul making in Romans 10:6-9?
7. Why are so many people concerned about winning approval from others?
8. What are two reasons that John states for the cowardly conduct of the religious leaders in John 12:42? Discuss how these two reasons affect us today.
9. What should be the goal of our ministry?
10. What happens to the individual who tries to please all the people, all the time?

Endnotes

1. Chuck Swindoll, *Encourage Me*, (Portland: Multnomah Press, 1982), p. 18.

2. Robert Schuller, *Self Esteem*, (Waco: Word Books, 1982), p. 15

7

the god of scientism

As I enter this chapter I need to make some preliminary observations before we begin. First, this chapter is in no way intended to discredit science, scientists, or technology. I have a great respect and appreciation for science and the advances it has made over the years. As I write this book I'm recovering from surgery and believe me — I'm thankful for modern technology!

I do believe, however, that it's a serious error to give God His walking papers simply because we can land a man on the moon or transplant a heart.

SCIENTISM DEFINED

Although the words science and scientism sound similar, in reality they are quite different. Science is a tool, a methodology for observing and obtaining information about ourselves and the universe in which we live. Scientism is a god. It is a philosophy *about* science and not science itself.

> The intellectual affirms that every intelligent man must respect science, regarding it as one of the means God has given us to discover His laws of nature, to conquer age-old ills, to explore the universe. . . . The idolatry consists in the worship of science as the panacea for all woes; in the myth that science is infallibly accurate, whereas all other knowledge is random and partial; in the belief that man can with security rely on science alone for salvation.[1]

Scientism is rarely espoused by scientists. Those who bow down to this god are those laymen who know just enough of what science can do that they believe given enough time, science will find all the answers to our problems. They look to science as the savior of the human race. Such confidence, however, is blind and misplaced.

NATURALISM

Scientism is based upon the presupposition called Naturalism. Naturalism is the belief that everything we see, everything we experience, every being, every event, is explainable by the total natural or material world. The universe exists as a closed system. Nothing or no one exists outside or apart from the material world. The existence of a supernatural realm is emphatically denied.

The late apologist, philosopher Francis Schaeffer wrote,

> The early scientists believed in uniformity of natural causes. What they did not believe in was the uniformity of natural causes in a "closed system." That little phrase makes all the

difference in the world. It makes the difference between natural science and a science rooted in a naturalist philosophy.[2]

It was the desire to better understand the Creator through His orderly universe that gave birth to science. Centuries later many scientists still embrace Christianity, or at least theism. Don't feel intimidated. You don't have to park your brains to be a Christian.

GOD'S DOUBLE REVELATION

The simplest and oldest way in which God has chosen to reveal Himself is through the created world (Rom. 1:20). The author of nature is also the author of the holy scriptures, and therefore, we can expect them to harmonize with one another when properly interpreted.

The psalmist David praised the Lord for His double revelation of sky and scripture, world and word, in Psalm 19. Six verses are dedicated to his revelation through nature, seven to his revelation through scripture and he closes the psalm with a prayer to his Rock and Redeemer.

The heavens and skies are personified in the first two verses. They are said to be in the process of constantly proclaiming God's glory. This proclamation is universal in nature (vs. 3). As a shepherd, David had many opportunities to lie under a star-studded sky and enjoy their luminous beauty (Psa. 8:3). Emerson perhaps described David's feelings during those inspired and extraordinary moments in the following words:

> The man who has seen the rising moon break out to the clouds at midnight, has been present like an archangel at the creation of light and of the world.[3]

This revelation through nature, as beautiful as it is, is still very limited. Man needed more. So God, through His Spirit, communicated propositional truth to His prophets. David praised the Lord for the preciousness of this more complete revelation not knowing that an even fuller revelation would one day majestically proceed forth from his loins — Jesus the Messiah.

Many have attempted to make theologians and scientists enemies. Such is not the case. If it is, then it is either bad science or bad theology that has caused them to be at odds. For God, the Creator of both world and word, is not an author of confusion.

This harmony between God's word and God's world was beautifully described by Sir Francis Bacon (1605) in the following way:

> Let no man think or maintain that a man can search too far or be too well studied in the book of God's Word or in the book of God's Works, divinity or philosophy, but rather let man endeavor an endless progression of proficience in both, only let man beware that they apply both to charity and not swelling.

SCIENCE HAS LIMITS

By the very nature of the discipline, science is limited in the scope of its study. The objects of its study must be able to be put through controlled empirical tests. In other words, it is limited to dealing with things that can be observed, touched, weighed, divided, handled, measured, etc. . . . Science does not deal with the metaphysical, supernatural, or moral realm of existence because such things cannot be empirically tested.

Secondly, the information gained through science can never in one sense be considered final or absolute. It will always be undergoing modification and re-examination as new empirical data is obtained. The best that science can give (and believe me I'm not knocking it) is a good working hypothesis.

> Scientists do not talk about certainties. The most venerable theory is subject to change without notice, if new discoveries undermine its foundations; but a theory represents some such judgement as "all available evidence up to now points this way."[4]

THINGS SCIENCE CAN'T DO

Science has no answer to what Jean Paul Sartre called the basic philosophic question — something is here rather than nothing is here. Why? Why is there a universe? Even if science reached a point where they understood everything *in* the universe the question "Why is there a universe to study" or "Why am I here to study it?" would remain unanswered. No amount of experimentation can answer that question because it lies outside the field of science. Science also cannot tell us about the supernatural due to the fact that their experimentation is confined to the natural.

Secondly, science cannot tell us what man "ought" to do. J. Robert Oppenheimer was the man in charge of the Los Alamos Project, which built and tested the first atomic bomb. He observed that,

> our work has changed the conditions in which men live, but the use made of these changes is the problem of governments, not scientists.[5]

Science itself is neutral. Good men can use its knowledge to help while bad men can use its knowledge to destroy. It's not the function of science to produce the good men. For that we must look elsewhere.

Thirdly, science cannot fill the void in the human heart. That void has to be filled with a Someone, not a something. Science is too cold and sterile to fill that desperate inner need. A scientist may be pleased by the fact that his research is blessing millions, but does the knowledge of that research itself — separated from its potential use — fill his need for meaning? Knowledge in any form, be it scientific or theological, won't fill the void. The void is filled only by Jesus Christ.

> I know *whom (not what)* I have believed and am persuaded that *he* is able to keep what I have committed to *him* until that day (II Tim. 1:12, italics mine.)

Man is longing for a personal relationship with his Creator. Neither science, nor scientific knowledge, is a substitute for that relationship.

CONSEQUENCES OF SCIENTISM

Ideas always have consequences. Let's look at three consequences that result from worshipping science as the god of your salvation.

1. *Determinism* — Those who worship at the altar of scientism view the universe as self-contained and closed. Therefore, everyone and everything can be explained by ongoing natural processes.

Man is merely a small cog trapped within the greater machine of the universe. As part of the machine, who he is and what he does, has already been determined. He's been preprogrammed by his upbringing and society to think and believe in certain ways. He's viewed as a product of his environment and of the chemical processes that go on within his body. Determinism views man as nothing more than a highly conditioned Pavlovian dog and, therefore, not responsible for his actions.

This is not the biblical view of man. Obviously environment, upbringing and society do play a part in shaping us. Ultimately, however, it boils down to how you choose to react to these outside variables and not the variables themselves. Many through the grace of God have risen above their environment while some who have had it all going for them blew it in a big way. Consider Adam and Eve. A reading of Ezekiel 18 teaches that we're not preconditioned or predisposed toward certain behavior. Character is a matter of personal choice. Our problem is not environment, but it's the attitude I saw expressed on a bumper sticker:

To err is human — To blame it on someone else is even more human.

2. *Dehumanization* — If man is nothing more than a part within the machine then I can treat my fellow man as a piece of automata. I can press the right buttons and manipulate him to do anything I desire, make him buy anything I wish him to buy. Control is the name of the game. So a few manipulators gain the control over the many.

The question is not *can* they do this, we see it done all the time, but rather *should* they treat their fellow man in such a dehumanizing, depersonalizing way. If man is just a part within the system manipulation poses no problem. If on the other hand, he has been endowed by his Creator with certain inalienable rights, then manipulation is clearly wrong.

3. *A Shift in Moral Values* — The Judeo-Christian ethic has been the basis for most of the laws in our society. It stresses the intrinsic value and worth of each human life, regardless of the quality of that life. But our society is changing and the reason is many have denied God's existence and abandoned His ethics as taught through scripture — and have accepted scientism. The result is a radical shift in moral values.

The following comes from an editorial in "California Medicine" written in September of 1970. It discusses the process of the erosion of the old ethic and the substitution of a new ethic.

> It will become necessary and acceptable to place relative rather than absolute values on such things as human lives, the use of scarce resources and the various elements which are to make up the quality of life or of living which is to be sought. . . . The process of eroding the old ethic and substituting the new has already begun. . . .

He then goes on and uses the issue of abortion as an example of this morality shift.

> Since the old ethic has not yet been fully displaced it has become necessary to separate the idea of abortion from the idea of killing, which continues to be socially abhorrent. The result has been a curious avoidance of the scientific fact . . . that human life begins at conception. . . . The very considerable semantic gymnastics which are required to rationalize abortion as anything but taking a human life would be ludicrous if they were not often put forth under socially impeccable auspices.

He then closes with this chilling bit of horror:

> One may anticipate further development of these roles as the problems of birth control and birth selection are extended inevitably to death selection and death control whether by the individual or by society, and further public and professional determinations of whom and when not to use scare resources.[6]

And who does he suggest should play a major role in determining who will live and die? You guessed it — the medical profession.

Let me be quick to say that many physicians and scientists would be shocked and appalled at such an article. But I appreciate his candor. It enables us to see the slippery slope that we as a society have started to tumble down. That article was written 17 years ago, yet by changing a few words it would sound like something circulated by Hitler's Third Reich. When society cuts itself off from God, the consequences are devasting.

THE CHRISTIAN AND MEDICINE

An entire book could be written concerning the Christian and modern medical technology or bio-medical decision making. That's not my purpose as I close this chapter. In relation to the Christian and medicine, one comment has to be made. I want you to understand that you are not confronted with an either/or choice of God or medicine. It's not either/or, but both/and.

In his book *Miracles*, C.S. Lewis reminds us of an often forgotten truth.

There is a sense in which no doctor ever heals. The doctors themselves would be the first to admit this. The magic is not in the medicine, but in the patient's body — in the *vis medicatrix naturae*, the recuperative or self-correcting energy of Nature. What the treatment does is to stimulate natural functions or to remove what hinders them. We speak for convenience of the doctor, or the dressing, healing a cut. But in another sense every cut heals itself: no cut can be healed in a corpse.[7]

As James closes his epistle, he writes,

Is anyone among you sick? Let him call for the elders of the church, and let them pray over him, anointing him with oil in the name of the Lord. And the prayer of faith will save the sick (James 5:14f).

Note that it is the prayer of faith that is credited for the healing of the individual. Oil was used in a number of ways in those days, one of which was medicinal (Isa. 1:6). The Samaritan poured oil into the wounds of the man robbed and beaten on the Jericho road (Luke 10:34). Josephus tells us that Herod when sick, bathed in oil (*Antiquities* 17:65). Therefore, James proposes that the Christian use the medicine of the day along with fervent prayer to the Great Physician.[8]

When I was in my late teens a brother in Christ suffered a massive heart attack while at work one Wednesday afternoon. When I arrived at church that evening the normal classes were cancelled. Everyone met in the auditorium for prayer. The doctors had informed this young man's family earlier in the afternoon that they had done all they could. There was nothing more which they could do for the patient. So the church began at 7:00 P.M. to offer up our heartfelt prayers to God asking him to spare the life of this young husband and father. The doctors said about 7:15

P.M. he took a sudden turn for the better, and they themselves had done nothing. He survived and went back to his family to live a full and happy life.

Luck? Coincidence? God forbid! It was the Heavenly Father, reaching down into time as a result of faith-filled prayer, who touched this young man with a healing hand.

Don't allow the god of scientism to influence the way you look and think about other people or about yourself. Don't depend on science as a panacea for all the ills of mankind. Scientism fosters a deterministic outlook on life, a dehumanized society and a radical shift in moral values. Science, my friend, can add years to your life; but only Jesus can add life to your years!

Questions and Answers

1. What is the difference between science and scientism? Do Christians have anything to fear from science? scientism?
2. What desire gave birth to science?
3. In this chapter, we discussed two ways in which God reveals Himself. What are they?
4. Are scientists and theologians natural enemies?
5. What are some limitations placed upon science?
6. What are some questions science can't answer?
7. Name some consequences of scientism. Discuss your answer in detail.
8. Is the Christian faced with an either/or proposition in regard to God or medicine?
9. Do your truly believe that God answers the prayer of faith today? Support your answer from scripture and perhaps some personal experience.

Endnotes

1. J.D. Thomas, *Facts and Faith*, (Abilene: Biblical Research Press, 1965), p. 102.

2. Francis Schaeffer, *Escape from Reason*, (Downers Grove: InterVarsity Press, 1968), p. 36.

3. Ralph Waldo Emerson, *On Man and God*, (Mount Vernon: Peter Pauper Press, 1961), p. 23.

4. Chad Walsh, *Campus Gods on Trial*, (New York: MacMillan Publishing Co., 1953), pp. 43-44.

5. Robert Baum, *Ethical Arguments for Analysis*, (Holt, Rinehart and Winston, Inc., 1973), p. 171.

6. *Ibid*, p. 172.

7. C.S. Lewis, *Miracles*, (New York: MacMillan Publishing Co., 1960), p. 140.

8. There are two Greek words for anoint. One meaning ceremonial anointing, like that of a priest or King; and the other a more general term. The latter is used in this context.

the god of materialism

The dyed in the wool materialist views matter as all that matters. According to him nothing else exists. He derives his self-esteem from what he has achieved and from the amount and quality of his possessions. His life's goal is to live in only the finest neighborhoods and frequent only the best restaurants. He wants to drive only the finest cars and wear only designer name clothing. Position and possession are the criteria by which he judges his value in life. Upward mobility becomes the driving force of life (I John 2:16).

The United States is infested with materialistic thought and people. Commercials zealously preach this gospel. We are told that products will solve all our problems. Got a problem attracting that certain someone? The solution will be found in buying the right toothpaste. Been passed over for the big promotion? Buy our deodorant and the vice-presidency will be yours! Often it takes one outside of our culture to see us as we really are — due to the fact that we can't see the forest for the trees. Alexander Solzhenitsyn addressed a large audience at Harvard University in 1978. In that speech he pointed out,

> We have placed too much hope in politics and social reforms, only to find that we were being deprived of our most precious possession: our spiritual life. It is trampled by the party mob in the East, by the *commercial one* in the West.

Many Americans continue to ignore their most precious possession. Instead they fashion and mold a golden calf to which they sacrifice their full devotion and dedication. This golden calf is the god of materialism. It's not my intention to encourage you to rush out and take a vow of poverty. Please keep in mind that it is possible for an individual to give up all of his possessions — move into a monastery, and still possess a covetous spirit. We often disown our things and never disown ourselves. The essence of my message is that Christians far too often are victimized by the seduction of wealth, power and prestige. Jeremiah proclaimed:

> Let not the wise man glory in his *wisdom*, let not the mighty man glory in his *might*, let not the rich man glory in his *riches*; but let him who glories, glory in this, that he understands and knows me, that I am the LORD . . .(Jer. 9:23f).

Man often worships the substitute trinity of wisdom, strength, and riches and not the heavenly Trinity of Father, Son and Holy Spirit. Jesus ceaselessly calls all of His disciples to develop a radically different attitude about these things.

> We are called to a simple life style in which wealth is utilized to bless the less fortunate. Power is abandoned in adopting of a lifestyle of servanthood and prestige is discarded in favor of Christian humility.[1]

Christians must learn to use wealth, power and prestige as means to an end of blessing others without allowing the means to become the ends in and of themselves.

THE LOVE OF MONEY

Newsweek magazine proclaimed 1984 as the year of the Yuppie — the young urban professional. Baby boomers by and large tend to see money as the root of all good. In fact, the editor of Money magazine said that "Money has become the new sex. It is the number one obsession among Americans."[2] As Paul told Timothy, "in the last days people will be lovers of themselves and lovers of money" (II Tim. 3:2).

Yet the same Bible that teaches us salvation in Jesus Christ also teaches us that "the love of money is the root of all kinds of evil" (I Tim. 6:10). Will we accept the first truth and disregard the second? Will we be guilty of the sin we accuse the denominational world of: the sin of going through the Bible cafeteria style picking and choosing what we like and ignoring the rest?

The media is filled daily with crimes that are spawned in greed. Robbery, embezzlement, fraud, blackmail, bribes and insider trading. The love of money will always cause you to compromise your values and principles. Paul indicates that this love for the material has caused, and will cause, Christians to compromise their faith (I Tim. 6:10b). As Christians, we are not to put our hope in wealth for security, but we are instead to place our hope in the One who owns the cattle on a thousand hills (I Tim. 6:17).

JESUS' TEACHING ON WEALTH

Our Lord Jesus was not a morbid ascetic. His first

recorded miracle, turning water into wine, kept the joy flowing at a wedding banquet. He felt at home at Levi's table rejoicing with this new disciple and his friends. My Lord's enemies accused Him of being a rabble rouser, "one who was a glutton and drunkard" (Luke 7:34). The gospel writers have portrayed Jesus as a man who enjoyed people and appreciated the things of this life.

On the other hand, the evangelists draw us a picture of Jesus as a man of simplicity. He had no earthly possessions. He was born in a borrowed manger, preached from a borrowed boat, ate the Last Supper in a borrowed room and was buried in a borrowed tomb. The Son of Man truly had "no place to lay his head" but at the same time He possessed "all authority in heaven and on earth" (Luke 9:58; Matt. 28:18). Our duty as Christians is to resolve for ourselves this dialectical tension between asecticism and an opulent life style.

> Two things I request of you (deprive me not before I die): remove falsehood and lies far from me; give me neither poverty nor riches — feed me with the food you prescribe for me; lest I be full and deny you, and say, "Who is the Lord?" Or lest I be poor and steal, And profane the name of my God (Prov. 30:7-9).

> I know how to be abased, and I know how to abound. Everywhere and in all things I have learned both to be full and to be hungry, both to abound and to suffer need (Phil. 4:12).

The prosperity gospel, the name it — claim it brand of Christianity proclaimed by many tele-evangelists, was unknown to my Lord. Jesus didn't come to make life easy, but to make men great!

Such greatness will never be obtained, however, if our

trust is misplaced. Therefore, Jesus spoke on many occasions about money and its influence upon us.

In the Sermon on the Mount, Jesus teaches us that we cannot serve both God and Money (Matt. 6:24). The word translated money is an Aramaic expression for wealth — Mammon. Jesus simply states that if material needs dominate our emotions it's absolutely impossible to be a faithful disciple.

Not only is it impossible to be a faithful disciple, but it brings with it a bondage: a bondage of anxiety and fear of the future. The Christian's walk is characterized by freedom from anxiety. He or she trusts that their heavenly Father is well aware of their needs and that He will provide for those needs (Matt. 6:25-34). A Christian filled with anxiety is demonstrating either a lack of faith in their Father, or they're being dominated by material needs and desires.

In the parable of the soils we find a warning concerning the deceitfulness of wealth and the desire for other things (Mark 4:1-20; Luke 8:1-15). The emphasis of the parable is not on the sowing, but on the soils, for each soil represents one of four ways people respond to the gospel. The path-soil hearers never believe while the shallow-soil hearers demonstrate a flash in the pan faith founded upon emotions not convictions. The good soil represents the faithful fruit-bearing saint. But what about the third soil?

The third soil represents one who has heard, believed and obeyed the gospel message. The thorny soil hearer is a Christian, but a Christian with a major problem. He or she never matures — never bears fruit — because he is overrun by the weeds of materialism. Life's worries, riches, and pleasures dominate his emotions, not the desire to please the Lord in all things (Luke 8:14). I'm afraid that our pews, and some of our pulpits, are filled with thorny-soil Christians. Perhaps this is a major reason for the kingdom's lack of growth. Jay Kesler reminds us:

> As families we must constantly analyze our faith. Are we just polite materialists rather than impolite materialists? Are we just secularists who don't swear and drink, or are we qualitatively different people?[3]

Jesus addresses the issue of materialism again in the parable of the rich fool (Luke 12:13-21). While discussing the person and work of the Holy Spirit in His ministry, Jesus was rudely interrupted by a man more concerned with the material than the spiritual. "Teacher," he said, "tell my brother to divide the inheritance with me." Jesus' response was sharp and to the point:

> Take heed and beware of covetousness, for one's life does not consist in the abundance of the things he possesses (Luke 12:15).

He then proceeds to illustrate this truth with a parable. Read it for yourself. The parable concerns a rich farmer who never saw beyond himself or this world. He hoarded his wealth giving no thought to his soul nor God. Jesus states that God calls such people "fools" because they ignored their most precious possession. Our Lord concludes in verse 21 by saying that destruction awaits anyone, disciples or otherwise, whose selfishness blinds them to spiritual reality. Here's where the rubber of faith meets the road of reality.

The apostle Paul has stated that a greedy person is an idolator and, therefore, has no inheritance in the kingdom of Christ, even if he is sitting in a pew every Sunday morning (Eph. 5:3-7; Col. 3:5-10). Covetousness is not a problem of the pocketbook, savings account or checking account. It's a heart problem. A man blessed with wealth may be a man after God's own heart while a man struggling to get by may be covetous to the core.

What then are we to do? The master gives the solution in Matthew 5:19-21 — put your treasure where you want your heart to be! Place whatever is of value to you; time, family, money or possessions into the kingdom of God and your heart will become centered in the kingdom.

It's been my experience that people who exercise spiritual principles in giving are not complacent or apathetic about the work of the church. It's also been my experience that people who sanctimoniously drop a dollar or two in the collection plate (when God has blessed them with much more) are cold, apathetic and indifferent toward the Lord, the reason being they are putting their treasure in something other than the kingdom of God. Reuel Lemmons wrote:

> Money comes nearer showing where the heart is than anything else. The sin of Ananias was not in what he gave, but in what he held back. The virtue of the poor widow in the temple was not in what she threw in, but in what she held back. It told on both of them and it tells on us. . . . Nothing indexes our character more than the way we handle our money. It is true with individuals or congregations.[4]

THE CONCEPT OF STEWARDSHIP

There is a difference in ownership and possession. If you rent and fail to recognize the landlord's ownership through monthly rent checks you'll eventually be evicted. Until you have the pink slip in your hand the bank owns the car you're driving even though it's in your possession. What is true in the physical realm regarding ownership and possession is also true in the spiritual realm.

The Bible states that, "The earth is the LORD'S and all

its fullness" (Psa. 24:1, 50:12). "The silver is mine and the gold is mine, says the LORD of hosts" (Hag. 2:8). We, the earth, and all that's in it owe our existence to God. We exist because He willed it. Therefore, God alone occupies the position of owner. We are simply stewards entrusted with the Master's possessions. Every good thing, including family, occupations and material possessions belong to Him, not us.

A failure to recognize the Lord's ownership over you and your possessions is tantamount to robbing God. We're robbing the Lord of the recognition and honor due Him.

Malachi closes the Old Testament canon. The recipients of Malachi's message have been back in Israel from exile for nearly a century. They've forgotten the lessons of the past and are once again failing to give God their best. They're offering the Lord sacrifices and gifts that were not suitable for their earthly governor (1:6-14). God was so incensed by their second-hand gifts that He told them to shut the temples and put out the sacrificial fire. According to the Lord — No worship was better than what they were offering.

In Chapter Three the Lord makes an angry accusation that mortal man is robbing God! (vv. 8-9). Such an accusation from the lips of Jehovah God should not be taken lightly. The Israelites were robbing Him not of material possessions (they were already His), but by failing to bring the tithe they were failing to recognize His ownership and robbing Him of His honor. Yet, He still desired to bless them and throw open the floodgates of heaven. The key to unlock those gates, however, lay in the hand of the worshipper (v. 10). The same holds true today. (Read II Corinthians 8-9). The question we must ask ourselves is not how much of my money am I going to give to the Lord, but rather how much of the Lord's money will I keep for myself!

WHY MATERIALISM FAILS TO SATISFY

An old Roman proverb stated that "Money is like sea water, the more you drink the thirstier you become." Those who worship at the altar of materialism have found that their desire for the newer and the better is voraciously insatiable. Solomon declared, "Whoever loves money never has money enough; whoever loves wealth is never satisfied with his income" (Eccl. 5:10, NIV).

Solomon was in a position to know the truthfulness of this claim. He was number one on Jerusalem's Fortune Five-hundred list. Here was a man wealthier than any other individual or monarch of his day. His tremendous wealth is described for us in I Kings 10:14-29. Silver was commonplace during his reign — only gold graced his palace. Yet this wealthy king discovered that if life is nothing more than scratching and clawing for more and more, satisfaction gradually disappears. He recognized that pursuing happiness through possessions meant the loss of contentment.

Have you noticed that most Americans live at the maximum standard of living their income will allow? Remember when you said, "If I only had this raise I'd be set. I could even put some money into savings." Then you got the desired raise and whamo! You didn't get ahead at all. Instead, you found new and better things on which you spent your raise. New debts, not new ground was gained.

Not only is this obsession insatiable, but it's also illusionary. In our saner moments we're painfully aware that money cannot buy love, health or happiness. It can't buy off the grim reaper. It fails to perform as promised. One day all humanity will stand before the Lord stripped down to their naked existence with no material link to their former lives. Then what? What will money and possessions do for you then?

Thirdly, the gnawing desire for more increases anxiety. The materialist is dominated by a paranoia that someone will steal what he possesses or in some way those possessions will be lost. An old Hasidic proverb reminds us that, "fear of misfortune is worse than the misfortune." As stated earlier in this chapter, anxiety concerning the future is an indication of either a lack of faith in our Father's ability to provide or evidence of a heart dominated by material desires.

Finally, the desire for wealth promotes selfishness. If you're convinced that money can do anything you'll likely do anything for money, even if it means ignoring the needs of others around you.

Luke informs us that the Pharisees were lovers of money (Luke 16:14). This self-centered drive led them to ignore the physical and financial needs of their parents. They even invented a spiritual justification for their tight-fisted self-absorption. If the parents approached them with specific needs, the pharisaical son would say that his money was Corban, a gift devoted to God, and therefore, he was unable to help them financially.

Sounds real spiritual doesn't it? Yet, after Mom and Dad would leave, they would dip into "God's money" and use it for themselves. Our Lord teaches us that such actions nullify God's word and make it void and worthless (Mark 7:9-13). And need I remind you that He still feels the same way about it today! Materialism always makes us near-sighted. Instead of blessing others, we're blind to the needs of others and our lives prove to be very hollow and inconsequential (I John 3:17f).

APPLICATION

Ken Samuel did an interesting study back in 1985.

Through analyzing the research of others, he found that the average North American congregation in our brotherhood has 97 active members. Thirty-two different family units comprise the average congregation. According to the 1980 census, the median annual income for an American family was $19,917. Now if each family tithed (the bare minimum under the old covenant) the average weekly contribution would be in the neighborhood of $1,225. Present estimates, however, indicate that the average congregation collects about $800. every Lord's Day.

What's being done with the other $425 per week? Most of it is being spent upon things other than the kingdom of God. Annually, that's a difference of $22,100 per congregation! Think of the missionaries, preachers, widows and orphans who could be supported with these funds.

God wants us to step out in faith and trust Him in our giving.

". . . prove me now in this," says the Lord of hosts, "If I will not open for you the windows of heaven and pour out for you such blessings that there will not be room enough to receive it" (Mal. 3:10).

Through serving the same congregation seven years, I've watched believers who've excelled in giving grow in grace and knowledge and be blessed abundantly by our Lord. I've watched others of a covetous spirit, who gave very little, shrivel up and die. The former gave themselves to the Lord while the latter were more concerned with what the Lord would give to them.

Is it possible that the North American church is bowing down to the almighty dollar rather than God? Will it be worth it if you gain the whole world — but in the end lose your own soul? The wise man was right; "Money can't buy everything": especially concerning matters eternal.

Question for Discussion

1. Are material things in and of themselves evil? When do they become an obstacle to the faith?
2. Name the three members of the world's trinity.
3. If Jesus were on this earth today, how do you think He would live? Describe His lifestyle.
4. Whom does Jesus call a fool?
5. Do you feel that Christians honestly believe that covetousness will keep them out of heaven? Explain your answer.
6. Explain the concept of Stewardship.
7. Give four reasons why materialism fails to satisfy.
8. Has this chapter caused you to re-examine your giving? If so, explain how.

Endnotes

1. Anthony Campolo, Jr., taken from *Christian Excellence*, by Jon Johnston, (Baker, 1985), p. 12.
2. Charles W. Colson, "A Call to Rescue the Yuppies," *Christianity Today*, (May 17,1985), p. 18.
3. Jay Kesler, *Christianity Today*, (October 18, 1985), p. 20.
4. Reuel Lemmons, *Firm Foundation*, (March 22, 1983), p.2

the god of hedonism

President Theodore Roosevelt summed it up well when he said, "The things that will destroy America are prosperity at any price, peace at any price, safety first instead of duty first, the love of soft living and the get rich theory of life." Not only will these things destroy our nation, but they will destroy the Lord's church as well.

The experienced missionary Paul warned the young evangelist Timothy about terrible times in the last days. He states that during that time people would be "lovers of pleasure rather than lovers of God" (II Tim. 3:4). The name for that philosophy of life is hedonism.

The word hedonism comes from the Greek word *Hedone*, which means pleasure. Hedonism is the doctrine that personal pleasure is the chief good and goal of life. Since pleasure implies freedom from pain, the hedonist attempts to avoid pain in any form and at all cost. The father of this popular philosophy was Epicurus. While in the metropolis of Athens, the apostle Paul publicly disputed with some of his disciples (Acts 17:12).

For one to be successful in the pursuit of happiness, he must be permitted to seek pleasure without fear of any reprisals or retaliation. Therefore, as far back as the third century B.C. men like Theodorus of Cyrene denied the existence of the gods. Without the ever watchful and restrictive eye of the gods, mortals were free to pursue pleasure in whatever form they desired. This, of course, led to open immorality and debauchery.

American society has also emancipated itself from all restraints and fear of reprisals as it shamelessly seeks personal pleasure and gratification. The fear of judgement does not restrain because the God of judgement has been declared non-existent. The fear of violating traditional values and morals has disappeared because moral absolutes have disappeared — everything is relative. The fear of social consequences for one's actions are diminished due to the fact that our present judicial system has no teeth. Prisons are overcrowded. Violators receive a slap on the wrist and then are released to pursue pleasure in whatever perverted form they please. Flagrant immorality and debauchery abounds. A quantum leap in moral deterioration is the awesome consequence of such hedonistic attitudes.

Let me remind you that we're discussing the abuse or the wrong pursuit of pleasure. Christians are called by the Lord to be sober, but not somber. The Bible mentions joy 164 times while the verb rejoice is found 191 times. The joy of the Lord is our strength! Therefore, Christians should be characterized by a joyful spirit (Neh. 8:10). In fact, the second fruit of the Spirit that He produces in our hearts is that of joy (Gal. 5:22). Our Father wants us to enjoy this life — however, we must guard against making pleasure, and not God, the ultimate goal of life. If we fail in this matter, we will find ourselves bowing before the god of Hedonism and holiness will be lost.

OUT OF MEN'S HEARTS

We live in a society desensitized to desecration. The media has played a major role in this desensitization process. The nightly news is filled with fast breaking stories concerning murder, rape, child abuse and other tragedies. Television programming is filled with immorality, adultery and fornication. Situations and events portrayed on the screen today would have appalled, shocked, and outraged the public twenty years ago. Today's viewer has grown numb through this exposure. Our eyes have become accustomed to viewing moral darkness.

The sexual revolution which began on the college campuses in the sixties and seventies has now penetrated the halls of America's high schools and junior high schools. One out of ten teenage girls becomes preganant each year leading to about one million teen pregnancies annually. The real tragedy, however, is that four-hundred thousand of those innocent infants will never take their first breath.[1] They'll be murdered by their mothers through abortion. Ten percent of America's teens have confessed to having intercourse by the time they reach age 13.[2] Since 1940 there has been an 800% increase in teen pregnancies among white school girls.[3] The result of all this is that very few churches in our country have not had to wrestle in one way or another with these social problems among their own membership. Desensitization is occurring within the church — and it must be stopped!

The sobering statistics mentioned above are the fruit of

an inward problem. To conform outward actions without a supernatural transformation of inward attitudes is merely putting new wine into old wine skins. Therefore, our focus needs to be on transforming the heart — for out of it flows the issues of life.

Jesus made it abundantly clear that "out of man's hearts, come evil thoughts, adulteries, fornications, murders, thefts, covetousness, wickedness, deceit, licentiousness, an evil eye, blasphemy, pride, and foolishness." All these come from inside a man — they flow out of a corrupt heart (Mark 7:21-23).

The word translated fornications is the Greek word *Porneia*. Our English term pornography is derived from this word. *Porneia* is a generic term. It includes any illicit or unlawful sexual conduct. It's an umbrella term that would include such things as adultery, fornication, incest, homosexuality or bestiality. All pornographic acts are the fruit of an unregenerate heart.

The word translated licentiousness (lasciviousness, KJV) is the Greek word *aselgia*. It implies an absence of restraint or discipline concerning the sexual appetite. Lewdness is to sex what gluttony is to eating. Both the physical and sexual appetites are God ordained desires which He placed within us, but we must not give free reign to these desires. We cannot afford to indulge every urge. The Spirit of self-discipline will assist Christians in determining when, where, and to what degree these desires should be satisfied (II Tim. 1:7). People however, with unregenerate hearts would argue "If it's pleasurable — do it!" "How could it be so wrong if it feels so right?"

JUST SAY NO

Several helpful programs have begun over the last few

years urging and encouraging young people to "Just say no" to things like drugs and alcohol. That advice, by the way, applies to us older folks as well. It's foolish to assume that we can teach our kids to say "No" to drugs and alcohol and not teach them to say "No" to illicit sexual activity. Through God's grace, young and old alike, have the power to say "No" to ungodliness and worldly passions (Titus 2:11f). Believers need to exercise that power today like never before. We must feel a divine duty to live lives of purity and holiness in the midst of our secular, hedonistic society.

THE CHRISTIAN AND SEXUALITY

Those who stand in the pulpit need to sound the clarion call demanding that sexual purity be practiced by God's holy people. Preachers have beat around the bush long enough. Sin must be identified as sinful. Church leadership can't continue to bury its head in the sand and hope that these accumulating problems will magically vanish in thin air.

At the same time, we must steadfastly love the individual trapped in sin. As we proclaim God's demands for holiness we must also proclaim God's willingness and ability to forgive. No one is beyond hope if they're willing to humbly and sincerely repent of their actions.

Do you not know that the unrighteous will not inherit the kingdom of God? Do not be deceived. Neither fornicators, nor idolaters, nor adulterers, nor homosexuals, nor sodomites, nor thieves, nor covetous, nor drunkards, nor revilers, nor extortioners will inherit the kingdom of God. *And such were some of you. But* you were washed, but you were sanctified, *but* you were justified *in the name of the Lord* Jesus and by the Spirit of our God (I Cor. 6:9-11, Italics mine).

111

Paul would strongly preach against sin and thankfully pronounce forgiveness in the same breath. We must learn to do the same.

The hedonistic sexual standards prevalent in our society have produced too many scarred and broken losers. An old platitude states "No action of any importance concerns only one person." Like throwing a stone in a pond, sexual activity touches an ever widening circle: the sex partner, the parents, the relatives, the friends and possibly a new life created through the union. The consequences of minimizing or rejecting God's moral standards are never pleasant.

PHYSICAL AND SOCIAL CONSEQUENCES

Consider the fact that there are twelve million cases of sexually transmitted diseases annually in this country alone. Diseases like herpes, a controllable but lifelong illness, or chlamydia, the major cause of sterility in young mothers, are common. The latter involves an inflamation of the fallopian tubes. During the infectious stages of this disease 80% of the women and 50% of the males show no symptoms whatsoever. Yet a young girl may suffer permanent sterility and never experience the joy of childbirth as a result of rejecting God's moral standards.[4] According to the Illinois State Medical Society 22,000 Illinois teens gave birth in 1986 and at least 500 of those births were to girls 14 and under.[5] The figures on a national scale are even more distressing.

Then of course there is the ever present threat of AIDS. In the case of this dreaded disease the outcome is not merely discomfort, but death. Dr. Edward J. Fesco, president of the Illinois State Medical Society states:

Sex education must first foster abstinence, by explaining the consequences of teen sex. . . . And it must clearly enumerate the medical and related health risks associated with sexual activity as well as drug abuse. There must be strong prevention-oriented messages from families, physicians and communities.[6]

And may I add the pulpit needs to take a more aggressive and assertive posture on these issues as well.

Consider the social consequences of abortion. Abortion in the United States has increased 15 fold since the infamous Roe v. Wade decision. One and a half million abortions are performed annually. Four-hundred thousand of which are performed upon teenage mothers. That means one innocent child is destroyed every 22 seconds — 4,000 destroyed every day in this, the so-called "land of the free."[7]

The social implications are dreadfully scary to say the least. A society that rationalizes the taking of the lives of innocent babies will also inevitably be able to rationalize the murder of other human beings at other stages of their lives. In an aricle in the Orlando Sentinel, Charles Reese suggested: Find yourself a pro-abortion argument and simply subsitute another word — AIDS victim, or retarded person for example — wherever fetus is used and notice how the argument follows uninterrupted.[8] What's the difference, my friend, in killing babies because they're babies and killing Jews because they're Jews? Not only do the unborn lose, but the adults lose as well as a result of hedonistic sexual standards.

THE EMOTIONAL CONSEQUENCES

I know of godly Christians who presently are faithfully

serving Jesus, but who suffer the deep emotional scars of an abortion in their past. God has forgiven these individuals through the blood of His Son and they're deeply thankful for that grace. But the scars still remain and the memories still haunt them.

So often a young woman who submits to an abortion is never told both sides of the issue. She receives only the biased pro-choice side and nothing more. In many cases they're not allowed to make an educated decision based upon weighing the facts of both sides. One reason is money. Abortion clinics reap an annual income in excess of 500 million dollars.[9] They have a vested interest. Young women are, therefore, exploited and taken advantage of and must, in many cases be viewed as victims themselves.

Another category of victims are the divorcees. We all are aware of the immeasurable emotional trauma which plays a part in divorce. Feelings of failure, anger, resentment, shattered dreams, promises broken, all cut deeply to the heart of those involved. I'm of the opinion that the rising divorce rate is also a symptom of a more deadly disease — that of worshipping false gods. God hates divorce and all the hellish effects it has upon the parties involved. God, however, does not hate the divorcee and neither must we (Mal. 2:16). They need our support and care as some painfully difficult life transitions are made.

A fact often overlooked is that teens, too, suffer real emotional loss when they breakup with a boyfriend or girlfriend. One survey revealed that only 14% of teenage sexual relationships last more than a year and about as many last only a week.[10] Serious emotional scarring occurs in such an environment where the most intimate act possible between two people is cheapened and degraded. God wants to spare us from these wounds by teaching sexual abstinence and chastity prior to marriage (Heb. 13:4). Those who become sexually active outside of marriage experience an addictive type of bondage to sex itself. Very few only have one or two sexual experiences of intercourse and quit. Only 6% of non-virgins surveyed had gone for more than a year since last having intercourse![11]

Paul instructs us that sex, outside of the bounds set by God, is a sin unique in its effect upon us. Those who sin sexually sin against their own body (I Cor. 6:18). I've watched young Christians who've made serious mistakes in this area weep and mourn over their sin only to find themselves getting involved in it once again at some later time. Hedonistic thinkers encourage us to give ourselves over to sensuality. The problem is that when we do, we become a slave to that lust and will indulge in every kind of impurity continually lusting for more unless heartfelt repentance takes place to break the momentum of this downward spiral (Eph. 4:19).

THE ETERNAL CONSEQUENCES

God is light and in Him is no darkness at all (I John 1:5). Even though God loves us, He will not, and cannot, fellowship with those who deliberately continue in sin. Even though Christians aren't sinless, we must learn to sin less. We cannot willfully choose to involve ourselves in acts which God's word clearly states are sinful.

God is not willing that any should perish. His last act of love is the promise of Hell. Through the fear of judgement He attempts to gain the attention of those who cannot be won through love alone. The issues we've been discussing are works of the flesh, and those who live like this will not inherit God's kingdom (Gal. 5:19-21). They are improper for

God's holy people (Eph. 5:3). As Paul states in I Thessalonians:

> It is God's will that you should be holy; that you should avoid sexual immorality; that each of you should learn to control his own body in a way that is holy and honorable, not in passionate lust like the heathen, who do not know God; and that in this matter no one should wrong his brother or take advantage of him. The Lord will punish men for all such sins, as we have already told you and warned you. For God did not call us to be impure, but to live a holy life. Therefore, he who rejects this instruction does not reject man but God, who gives you his Holy Spirit (4:3-8, NIV).

Don't be deceived my friend. God cannot be mocked. You will reap what you sow.

THE CHRISTIAN RESPONSE

Let me share six guiding principles which may help you in your struggle against the god of Passion.

1. *Learn to say "No" and mean it. Titus 2:12*
While in an alien, hostile environment, Daniel and his three friends purposed in their hearts that they'd not defile themselves (Dan. 1:8). You, too, can make the same choice. It's one of Satan's lies which states "Everyone is doing it." My friend — everyone is not doing it!
William S. Banowsky wrote concerning this matter:

> Nothing is more absurd than a technical virgin. Christ's cutting remark about straining the gnat and swallowing the camel, humps and all, perfectly fits such moral manipulation. This myth has helped to open the floodgates to a tidal wave of noncoital promiscuity.[12]

2. Avoid the appearance of evil. I Thessalonians 5:22

Don't see how close you can get without "actively" getting involved. Parents watch highly questionable, if not downright ungodly, movies on their TVs or VCRs, and then wonder why their children fail to demonstrate strong moral values. Moses warned his children not to "bring an abomination into your house" (Deut. 7:26) and the principle still applies! Ask God's help in monitoring your listening and viewing habits. Don't program your brain with junk. Don't allow your mind to become a garbage dump.

3. Flee when necessary. II Timothy 2:22

It takes courage to struggle against the current. Some teens were out at a restaurant when one in the group suggested that they all go to a popular night spot known to have a bad reputation. One young Christian replied, "You'd better take me home first." A friend snickered mockingly, "Afraid your father will hurt you?" "No," she said confidently, "I'm not afraid he'll hurt me, I'm afraid I might hurt my father."

Love for God will cause us to flee when necessary.

4. Pray for strength to be a godly example. I Timothy 4:12,16

We must be concerned about our example and influence upon others. You may be the only Bible your lost friend may ever read. Share God's message with both life and lip. His word convicts, but our lives convince those to whom we speak that we earnestly believe what we say.

5. Learn to share your fears, frustrations and failures. Galatians 6:2.

Parents, listen to your children. Young people, your parents can't read your minds. We all need trustworthy spiritual advisors to whom we can turn for a listening ear or for godly advice.

6. *Enjoy and nurture the relationship with your spouse.*
I am to view my spouse as an extension of myself. That is what the Bible means by the phrase "the two shall become one flesh." We need to learn to seek our spouse's highest good spiritually, emotionally and sexually. When both partners adopt this attitude — marriage will be as our Father intended and we'll experience His richest blessings in our relationship.

Questions for Discussion

1. What does the term hedonism mean? Does this describe the philosophy of many Americans?
2. How should the church respond to unwed mothers? Remember we hate the sin *not* the sinner.
3. What gives us the power to say, "No!"?
4. Describe the emotional consequences of sexual promiscuity. Does it affect more than just one person? Explain your answer in detail.
5. Discuss the six guiding principles for the Christian.
6. How can parents and teens dialogue on this important topic? Share some ideas.

Endnotes

1. Warren E. Leary, Science writer for the Associated Press, (December 10, 1986).

2. *USA Today*, (3/29/85 — 3/31/85).

3. Charles Colson, *Christianity Today*, (January 16, 1987), p.72.

4. Tim Stafford, "Our Latest Sexual Fantasy," *Christianity Today*, (January 16, 1987), p. 24.

5. Dr. Edward J. Fesco, President of the Illinois State Medical Society, Interview and Article, (November 26, 1987).

6. *Ibid*.

7. Don Wildman, *National Federation for Decency Journal*, (October, 1984), p. 16.

8. Charles Reese, *Orlando Sentinel*, May 1, 1987.

9. *Don Wildman, op.cit.*, p. 16.

10. Tim Stafford, *op. cit.*, p. 25.

11. *Ibid.*, p. 25

12. William S. Banowsky, "Sex and Morality," *Twentieth Century Christian*, (March 1969), p. 21.

10

the god of legalism

The ancient Greeks told a legend that today is used to signify two equal but opposite dangers. According to the legend, two overwhelming dangers awaited the ships that passed through the Straits of Messana between Sicily and Italy. On the Italian side dwelt a hideous six-headed monster, by the name of Charybdis. This creature devoured any ship that strayed too close to its shores. Opposite Charybdis, on the Sicilian coastline, was a large whirlpool, that three times daily swallowed the waters of the sea and any vessels caught in its deadly currents. Thus to safely navigate the straits of Messana, you had to cautiously sail between Scylla and Charybdis.

Extremes tend to beget extremes. In running from Rome some unintentionally run past Jerusalem. David Lipscomb sounded this warning:

> In running from one extreme we so often run to the opposite. From the extreme of sacrificing truth for the sake of

union, many substitute their own narrow, imperfect, and exclusive ideas for the law of God. . . . Everything that admits what God excludes is sectarianism. Everything that excludes what God admits is sectarianism.[1]

In his last public discourse, our Lord Jesus warned the multitudes and His disciples concerning the dangers of extremism (Matt. 23:1). Christ criticized the religious leaders because they "neglected the weightier matters of the law."[2] All of God's truths are equally true, but they are not all equally important. Jesus Himself stated that Deuteronomy 6:4f. and Leviticus 19:18 ranked number one and two in their importance. In fact, He said, "There is no commandment greater than these" out of the 613 laws recorded in the Pentateuch (Mark 12:28-41).

LEGALISM DEFINED

The extreme that we are concerned with in this chapter is that of legalism. Although not a word found in the Bible, it is a concept found throughout its pages. *Webster's New World Dictionary of the American Language*, defines legalism in theology as "the doctrine of salvation by good works."[3] Jesus dealt with this issue in the familiar parable of the Pharisee and the tax collector. This parable was directed toward those who, "trusted in themselves that they were righteous" (Luke 18:9).

Legalism is not to be confused with faithful, heartfelt obedience to our Lord's commands. It's a fact of life that if you sincerely trust and love Jesus; you will joyfully keep His commandments (John 14:15). Legalism, however, is trusting in your ability to keep God's commands as the way to obtain justification and right standing with God. In the first instance, you trust Jesus for your happiness and security. In the second, your trust for happiness and security rests in your own performance. This is not just a play on words. It's a serious matter; a matter of spiritual life or death.

You who attempt to be justified by law; you have fallen from grace (Gal. 5:4).

Man often hides his pride and self-sufficiency beneath the godly robes of religion and morality. When our trust slowly shifts from Jesus as our justifier, to personal performance as our justifier, our godly robes begin to unravel. The tradition of bringing flowers to a funeral initially began as a way to mask or cover up the smell of the death. But no matter how beautiful the flowers are or how fragrant the room may be, dead is dead. The same holds true spiritually.

DEPICTION OF LEGALISM – THE PHARISEES

The Pharisees are first mentioned by Josephus in connection with the events of the second century B.C. Jospehus defines the Pharisees as a body of Jews who profess to be more religious than the rest and who explain the laws more precisely.[4] In other words they claimed to be the true interpreters of the law of Moses: the ones who cornered the market on God's truth.

The Pharisees had a deep reverence for the Scripture. They also believed that the law of Moses had to be properly interpreted and applied to their present day and age. Their interpretations were known as oral traditions; and were equally binding and equally authoritative as the word of God from which they came. For instance, how was the Jew to understand Exodus 20:8, that no work was to be done on the Sabbath? The Pharisaic interpretations and oral traditions concerning that verse are found in written form in the Mishnah. Here are some examples of the minute punctiliousness that they practiced as a result of legalism.

1. A Jew could tie a knot on the Sabbath if he could untie it with one hand.
2. If death threatened on the Sabbath you could call a physician, but a fracture could not be attended to until the next day.
3. If you sprained a hand or a foot, you couldn't pour water on it on the Sabbath. That would be work.
4. A woman couldn't look in a mirror on the Sabbath. She might see a grey hair and be tempted to pull it out. That would be work.

The Pharisees were deeply concerned about maintaining their Jewish identity. The Jews had been conquered on numerous occasions throughout their history. Each conquest brought with it new cultures, new religions, new customs, languages, dress, etc. . . . The Pharisees were determined to save their nation from the corrupting influences of those Gentile cultures. They didn't want the people of God to be absorbed or assimilated into those foreign cultures. Therefore, distinctive outward signs, symbols, rituals and customs were bound upon the people in an attempt to distinguish the faithful and set them apart from the rest of humanity. Even their name, "Pharisee" meant one set apart.

They viewed themselves as the guardians and protectors of the true Jewish faith. That's why Jesus infuriated them! Jesus downplayed the need for their external rules and regulations and scripturally showed their official interpretations to be wrong (Matt. 9:10-13; Mark 2:18-22, 7:1-23,

12:35-37; Luke 6:1-5, 13:10-17). The religious leaders were afraid that if Jesus' way of thinking prevailed, there may come a day when there would be "neither Jew nor Greek, neither slave nor free, neither male nor female" (Gal. 3:8). Such a concept, they could not tolerate.

The Talmud distinguished seven types or classes of Pharisees, one of which was the "Reckoning Pharisee."[5] This individual constantly asked himself the question "What duty must I do in order to balance any omissions?" His way of life was one of balancing the scales. He believed that if on the day of Judgement his good deeds outweighed his sins and shortcomings, then God would usher him into Abraham's bosom. However, if the scales were tipped to the side of his sins, then eternity would be spent with the devil and his angels. This is legalism pure and simple. This is the attitude that is robbing many Christians of peace and filling them with doubt. This is the attitude which prompts the troubled believer to say, "I don't know if I've done enough." It causes others to view themselves as God's gift to the church, looking down their spiritual noses at fellow-believers who don't do as they do or believe as they believe. The words of this poem capture the essence of this attitude.

> Believe as I believe, no more, no less;
> That I am right and no one else confess.
> Feel as I feel — think only as I think,
> Eat what I eat, and drink but what I drink.
> Look as I look, do always as I do, and
> Then — and only then — I'll have fellowship
> With you.
>
> Author Unknown

THE DOCTRINE OF JUSTIFICATION BY FAITH

Legalism is an unbearable yoke, one from which only

Jesus can set us free.

> Come to me all you who labor and are heavy laden, and I will give you rest. Take my yoke upon you and learn from me, for I am gentle and lowly in heart, and you will find rest for your souls (Matt. 11:28f).

> Now therefore, why do you test God by putting a yoke on the neck of the disciples which neither our fathers nor we were able to bear? (Acts 15;10).

> Stand fast, therefore, on the liberty by which Christ has made us free, and do not be entangled again with a yoke of bondage (Gal. 5:1)

The epistles make it clear that we are not saved by our works (Eph. 2:8). We are not saved by what we do, but by what Jesus did and presently is doing on our behalf (Heb. 7:25). The cross of Calvary stands as proof of our desperate condition before God, "for if righteousness comes through the law, then Christ died in vain" (Gal. 2:21).

Paul wrote the book of Galatians to deal with this problem of legalism. After their initial conversion to Christ, false teachers moved in and troubled these new Christians (Gal. 1:6f). These teachers emphasized human effort as the means by which Christian perfection could be obtained (Gal. 3:3). The saints in Galatia were taking their eyes off Christ's perfection and focusing their attention on their own performance and practice. This chain of events led to the writing of the letter. Paul argues in Chapter Three that the legalist has misunderstood the nature of law.

1. Law Cannot Justify, 3:11

The legalist, by trying to be justified by his works, demonstrates a distorted understanding of the sinner. "By the deeds of the law no flesh will be justified in His sight, for by the law is the knowledge of sin" (Rom. 3:20). "For by the works of the law no flesh shall be justified" (Gal. 2:16).

For example, by looking in a mirror we're able to see the dirt on our face that we cannot see on our own. The mirror's function is to reveal filth, not cleanse it. A plumbline can't straighten a crooked wall, it merely reveals the fact that the wall is crooked. The sign which reads: No Swimming — Sharks; doesn't rid the water of sharks: but thank God for the sign!

The purpose of the law was to reveal those thoughts and actions which are not in harmony with God's holy character. We must turn to something, or someone, other than law in order to obtain spiritual cleansing and justification for our sins. This cleansing was provided to those under the law, but not on the basis of their works. Righteousness was obtained through faith in God as the justifier, not in personal performance or commandment keeping (Gal. 3:11, Hab. 2:4).

2. Law Demands Flawless Obedience, 3:12

The righteousness that is by the law states, "The man who does them shall live by them" (Lev. 18:5, Rom. 10:5). Under the law life is totally dependent upon ability and performance. As long as a person "does" the law perfectly, life is his. But woe to him who fails!

"God is light and in him is no darkness at all" (I John 1:5). He cannot look upon or fellowship wickedness, because its not in harmony with his character (Hab. 1:13). The legalist, or any person who is 99.44% pure is an ungodly person, because God is 100% light. This individual may be religiously and morally far superior in comparison to his fellow man. In comparison to God, however, he is ungodly; a sinner standing in need of grace. Spiritual life then is possessed in only one of two ways; perfect performance or pardoning grace.

3. Law Condemns The Violator, 3:10

Since the keeping of the law preserved life, the breaking of the law brought death. The commandment which was to bring life, Paul found to bring death (Rom. 7:10). God's curse falls upon *everyone* who doesn't do *everything* that God's holiness and law requires (Deut. 27:26).

Imagine that a business firm in L.A. employs a man, gives him months of intensive training and then sends him to Chicago. Monthly he receives a salary check from the home office. At the end of the year his supervisor discovers that all the time this man was in Chicago he was actually working for another firm, although he continued to cash the checks from L.A. The law would declare this man a thief.

This is the case of every sinner. God the Creator gives us life and sends us into His world. While on this earth our Heavenly Father provides us with the air that we breathe, food, water, shelter — in short every perfect gift comes from Him (James 1:16). We then rebelliously choose to serve another master, another god; while continuing to use God's gracious gifts. Such an individual is as guilty of robbing God as was the employee from L.A.

Good works cannot save. Our good works are merely the normal, minimal response the creature should give to his Creator. Our good works are merely giving God the honor He is due.

What is it that we owe God, by virtue of the fact that we owe our very existence to Him? Simply this — that every thought and every action be subject to the will of our Creator. Everyone who perfectly pays this debt never sins. All who fail to pay, sin.

Satisfaction for sin cannot be obtained by our good works. Good works are merely what is expected and that expectation has already been violated! Are we going to earn God's favor by merely doing what He expected us to do in the first place?

JESUS OUR SATISFACTION

Paul states the good news when he writes, "Christ has redeemed us from the curse of the law, having become a curse for us" (Gal. 3:13). In the famous words of Athanasius, "The Son of God became man so that men might become sons of God." Jesus became sin so that His righteousness might be imputed to us through faith (II Cor. 5:21).

In Jesus' sacrifice God's wrath and divine justice is satisfied. "He shall see the travail of his soul, and be satisfied" (Isa. 53:11). This is what the New Testament writers mean when they speak of propitiation (Rom. 3:25; I John 2:2, 4:10). At the cross, God maintained His honor and justice. A kingdom that never punished its lawbreakers could not exist. Law and order, authority and society itself could not exist. Anarchy would reign. To punish without mercy especially when all are guilty would also destroy that society.

At Calvary, God's authority and justice are preserved. At the cross we see the ugly, hideous consequences of our own sin and rebellion. The deep, painful, punishment inflicted upon Jesus was for your sin and mine.

Surely he has borne our griefs and carried our sorrows; Yet we esteem him stricken, smitten by God and afflicted. But he was wounded for our transgressions, he was bruised for our iniquities; the chastisement for our peace was upon him, and by his stripes we are healed (Isa. 53:4f).

Such punishment awaits all the unrepentant, all who fail to acknowledge their need for a Savior, and all who try to perfect themselves through human effort. The Christian's response to the cross is to gladly walk in the good works which God prepared beforehand for us to do. Not in order to "get saved" but because we are saved!

CONCLUSION

Those who strive to be justified by law have literally made a god out of their works. They believe that salvation is incumbent upon them properly putting all the pieces of the doctrinal puzzle in their proper place. They have failed to understand that any system of law, be it moral or religious, 1. Cannot justify; 2. Demands flawless obedience; 3. Condemns the violator. They've also overlooked the fact that good works are the minimal, normal response of the creature to his Creator. You don't earn points by merely doing what's expected of you.

One final thought: legalism is built upon a repression of inner guilt feelings.

> Struggling to keep potentially guilt-producing thoughts from awareness, the legalistic person maintains a continued focus on eternal actions, works and effort. This helps shift attention from hidden, but unacceptable, attitudes and feelings.[6]

If you're troubled by such feelings, don't bow to the idol of good works. You need to go to the cross, look at the price He paid for you; and hear the words of the apostle Paul, "There is therefore now no condemnation to those who are in Christ Jesus" (Rom. 8:1).

Questions for Discussion

1. How does Jesus' statement "Blind guides who strain out the gnat and swallow the camel" relate to the concept that there are weightier matters of the law?
2. Obedience to what two commands should serve as our rule of life? Explain why these are sufficient.
3. Josephus described the Pharisee as one who explained God's laws more precisely and felt more religious than the rest. Do you see similar attitudes demonstrated by the church? Is such an attitude helpful or a hindrance to others?
4. What are three aspects concerning law that the legalist fails to understand?
5. Why is it impossible for good works to save?
6. What lessons do we learn about God's justice when we look at the cross?
7. What ways do you see Christians trying to "balance the scales" in their religious life?
8. Describe actions or attitudes which would indicate a legalistic mindset.
9. What might lead a person to become legalistic concerning his faith?

Endnotes

1. David Lipscomb, *Gospel Advocate*, (1909), p. 46.

2. It's interesting to note that Jesus implies by this statement that within His Father's divine revelation, there are matters and issues of lesser importance. The prophets also reminded God's people of this truth on numerous occasions (Hosea 6:6; Amos 5:21-24; Micah 6:6-8).

4. Josephus, "The Wars of the Jews," *Josephus*, (Grand Rapids: Kregal Publications, 1977), p. 434.

5. James Orr, *The International Standard Bible Encyclopedia*, (Grand Rapids: Wm. B. Eerdmans Publishing Co., 1976), Vol. 4, p. 2365

6. S. Bruce Naaramore, *No Condemnation*, (Grand Rapids: Academie Books, 1984), p. 39-40.

the god of traditionalism

The purpose of the preceding chapters has been to identify rival gods not merely for the purpose of identification, but so that iconoclasm can take place. These gods hinder our walk in holiness and keep us from being all that our Father created us to be. In my opinion, the god which stifles and strangles the spirituality of most saints is the god of traditionalism. As you read this chapter, please keep in mind that I'm primarily addressing the body of Christ and not other religious institutions.

TRADITIONS CAN OUTLIVE THEIR PURPOSES

Bismarck of Germany once made an official visit to the Czar of Russia. When he arrived at the Czar's palace he noticed a military guard standing in the middle of the lawn for no apparent reason. Bismarck inquired of the Czar concerning this soldier's significance. The Russian honestly replied that he didn't know himself — but as long as he could remember a guard stood at that spot, 24 hours a day. The Czar's curiosity was aroused by his visitor's question. He asked other staff members and found that no one knew the reason for the sentry. The Captain of the guard began sifting through old court records and finally discovered the answer.

Several decades earlier the Czar's grandmother noticed a beautiful wild flower blooming in the palace lawn. Afraid it might be destroyed, she ordered a guard to protect the flower from careless feet. The little flower had long since died, but the order was never rescinded. Up until now no one questioned the tradition. For generations soldiers stood at that spot 24 hours a day, 7 days a week, 52 weeks a year — for absolutely no reason.

That incident graphically illustrates the need for Christians to question and challenge their religious traditions in order to establish whether or not they stand on a biblical foundation. John Stuart Mill wrote:

There is a great difference between presuming an opinion to be true because with every opportunity for contesting it, it has not been refuted, and assuming its truth for the purpose of not permitting its refutation.[1]

THE TRUTH SHALL SET YOU FREE

Only through a full and free surrender to the facts is genuine freedom possible. Only "the truth shall make you free" (John 8:32). A scientist must be able to objectively look at the factual results of his experimentation and without manipulation allow those facts to lead him to an accurate conclusion. The same holds true spiritually.

In John 8, Jesus has gone up to the Feast of Tabernacles. He has claimed to be the one who can quench our unquenchable thirst for meaning and fulfillment (7:37). He has announced Himself as this dark world's light of life (8:12). Many miraculous signs, showing evidence of His Father's presence, had already been performed (7:31) and His following was increasing in size. Many put their faith in Him (8:30).

The discussion which follows is addressed to this group who had already believed on Him. Although they believed, it's obvious from the discussion that they possessed a distorted and warped view of Jesus. Jesus proclaimed that even though they were religious, they belonged to their father the devil! You may wonder, how could this be.

If you believe in Jesus as the Messiah and if your concept of *who* God's Messiah is, and *what* God's Messiah is to do, is wrong, then that concept will discolor and distort your view of Jesus. You'll look at Him through the colored glasses of your distorted concept and fail to see Him as He is. On the other hand, if you place your trust and faith in Jesus, gladly surrendering to His truth, then He will instruct you concerning the person and work of the Messiah.

We must first believe in Jesus and allow Him to interpret the truth concerning God and His commandments. If we come to Him with preconceived notions concerning God, the nature of sin, His word or His church, then we fail to give Jesus a proper hearing and we have no room for His word of truth (v. 37). That's a truly dangerous position to be in. In fact, many erroneous presuppositions and preconceived ideas make us unable to hear what Jesus has to say to us (v. 43).

Because the Jews were steeped in certain traditional interpretations of the law and the promises, they were unable to accept Jesus' teaching since His teachings clashed with their interpretations. Today members of our Lord's church need to constantly remember that we haven't cornered the market on truth. We, too, can fall into the same trap the Pharisees and others fell into.

How often do we make Scripture the prisoner of our own interpretation.[2] We come to the Bible with the conviction that we already possess the true understanding of Scripture and, therefore, God's Spirit is unable to instruct us — unable to give us new insights into truth and deeper fellowship.

We need to be open for new instruction from our Father every time we open His book.

> To read the Bible as God's word, one must read it with his heart in his mouth, on tip-toe, with eager expectancy in conversation with God.[3]

Truth has nothing to fear from inquiry. Yet if we attempt to suppress or destroy disturbing truth we're doing the Devil's work and not God's (v. 44).

Too often we're willing to let someone else tell us what the Scriptures teach without studying them for ourselves (Acts 17:11). I'm not indicating that we shouldn't seek advice — "in the multitude of counselors there is wisdom." I am saying, however, that if we determine truth merely by brotherhood consensus — we have missed the mark. Truth is truth even if it's a minority of one! Thomas Campbell understood this critical principle:

> It is not the voice of the multitude, but the voice of truth, that has power with the conscience; that can produce rational conviction and acceptable obedience. A conscience that awaits the decision of the multitude, that hangs in suspense for the casting vote of the majority, is a fit subject for the man of sin.[4]

David Lipscomb wrote:

> A truth seeker realizes all parties hold some element of truth. Usually each party holds and emphasizes some particular truth in a way of its own. He will approach every teacher and every system as holding and cherishing some truth that he desires to learn and hold. He will feel kindly toward all. He who is most willing to receive truth from others is the most effective teacher of truth to others. [5]

Are you a truth seeker? Are you willing to humble yourself before Jesus the Master teacher as a small child and be taught by Him? Are you zealously following truth wherever it may lead or are you content to simply perpetuate your own spiritual species? The way of holiness is the way of truth. The way of holiness means a surrender to Him who is the embodiment of truth (John 14:6), and not a surrender to the god of traditionalism.

FORMALIZING THE TRUTH

Students of church history know that there are discernible patterns of growth that religious movements undergo in order to become socially acceptable. These changes can be clearly seen in the various branches of the sixteenth century Protestant reformation movement. They also can be seen in the nineteenth century Restoration movement. H. Richard Neibuhr has defined these stages as the: 1. Period of the Man; 2. Period of the Movement; 3. Period of the Message; and 4. Period of the Monument. With each step the movement's effectiveness is gradually diminished, although it still may grow numerically it ultimately dies a quiet dignified death.

I'll never forget the impact this concept had upon me

when I first confronted it in college. We were studying Sociology of Religion. What was particularly disturbing to me was that the textbook, *Religion in Contemporary Society*, was using what they termed the Campbellite movement as an example of this growth pattern. The words especially stung because I knew that much of what they were saying was absolutely on target:

> Religious movements do not stand still; they either grow or wither. If the group continues, it generally faces a crisis of leadership as the original leader or leader dies. . . . The tendency is to resort to what is called "traditional" leadership. That is, there are still no rules or creeds, but the teachings of the charismatic leader become "policy" and interpretations of those teachings become the benchmark for the group.[6]

As our movement moved into the second and third generation, a greater emphasis was placed on orthodoxy (right doctrine) rather than orthopraxy (right living). The reason being, it made it easier to identify a person as "one of us" by where he stood on the issues or if he willingly gave assent to certain doctrinal interpretations from Scripture.

> If a religious group continues into the second and third generation, it will take on a much more formal style of leadership. . . . Now the rules, laws, and strictures against which the movement may have first protested become a part of the group's life. Although a variety of terms may be used to disguise the fact, the movement is now established, its policies "routinized," and there are official rules and channels for making decisions.[7]

This formalization of doctrine becomes a creed, whether written or unwritten. A creed is nothing more than a setting forth of doctrinal teachings which a particular religious body has deduced from Scripture. We may disagree with the conclusions reached or the logic used — but such is the nature of a creed, discipline, or confession.

The restoration fathers were not opposed to the publishing for information's sake concerning what they believed or practiced. This published work would be, by definition, a creedal statement. For instance, the well known tract "What is the Church of Christ" is a statement of belief concerning what we feel the Scripture teaches on various topics.

What the restoration leaders stoutly refused to do, however, was to make these statements of belief binding and authoritative upon all. It was the Bible, and not inferences and deductions from the Bible, which they held as the sufficient rule for faith and practice. Barton W. Stone wrote in 1835:

> The Pope is the foundation of the Papal establishment. The Pope's explanation of the Scriptures is paramount to the Scriptures themselves. Protestantism among the various sects is "Popery without a Pope." The creed, discipline or confession supplies the place of the Pope and is equally infallible, though in word denied. The explanation of the Scriptures in this book is paramount to the Scriptures themselves.[8]

Have we allowed our explanation of the Scriptures to become as authoritative as the Scriptures themselves? Have we become sectarian in our attitude as we bow down before the god of traditionalism? David Lipscomb defined a sectarian as one, "who takes for granted that everything his party holds is right and everything the other party holds is wrong. Hence party lines define his faith and teaching." I know of many Christians who sadly fall into this category.

ARE THERE NO ABSOLUTES?

Jesus is the great Fact to whom we must surrender. He is

the revelation, embodiment and interpreter of truth. Christians are converted to a person — not to a set of propositions. Jesus is our Source of Unity. His cross is the banner lifted high that His troops rally around. As we draw closer to Jesus, we will in turn be drawn closer to one another. The result will be an indivisible unity centered upon Christ.

In Matthew's account of the great commission we find recorded our marching orders issued from the Captain of our Faith (Matt. 28:18-20). As we go forth making disciples of all nations, His orders were not to teach them "everything I have commanded you." His orders were to teach them "to obey everything I commanded you." Our Lord is deeply concerned with orthopraxy! He wants a body of believers who will enflesh the message of God's salvation as He Himself did.

Does this mean that the early church had no doctrinal standards for unity? Of course not. Ephesians, chapter four, lists seven essentials that are non-negotiable. They bestow upon the church a uniqueness which distinguishes her from other religious bodies. These essentials are: One body, One Spirit, One hope, One Lord, One faith, One baptism, and One God.

People will never fully agree upon specifics. They can, and must however, agree upon the seven major truths of the revealed faith and live lives consistent with these truths. The restoration leaders realized that division in the body of Christ is a direct result of transforming personal opinions, which are not plain statements of Scripture, into tests of fellowship. Campbell stated in the Declaration and Address:

> Many of the opinions which are now dividing the church had they been let alone, would have long since been dead and gone; but the constant insisting upon them as articles of faith and terms of salvation, have so beaten them into the

minds of men, that in many instances they would as soon deny the Bible itself as give up one of these opinions.[9]

That applies to us! We dare not make anything a test of fellowship or salvation for which we do not have a clear and plain "thus saith the Lord." Many problems within the church could be eliminated if we would only practice the motto of the movement, "In essentials unity; in opinions libery; in all things love" (see Romans 14).

I've experienced the joy of working with other brothers in Christ who held differing opinions on various topics like: church co-operation, the work of the Holy Spirit, the function of elders, the nature of worship, the coming of the Lord, etc. . . . We worked harmoniously side by side serving the same Lord. We were able to openly, and in a brotherly fashion, discuss our differences and glean from one another. Many times we agreed to disagree — but we always did so with respect for each other.

I've also experienced the frustration of working with brethren who, like the world, tried to press you into their mold. They desired uniformity, not unity. They felt threatened by anyone who was different. They were wary of anyone who offered new insights or alternative interpretations from the Bible. To be one of them you had to assent to their unwritten creed. You tell me: Which group possessed the spirit of the New Testament Christianity? Which group demonstrated the spirit of sectarianism? Which group would you want to be a part of?

CONCLUSION

Each generation must make its faith its own. We must

approach Jesus through His word and be willing to be taught of Him. Those who worship at the altar of traditionalism are not willing to be taught they already have the answers.

During the dark days of the civil war, a clergyman approached President Lincoln. He said that he hoped "the Lord was on our side." Lincoln disagreed. He explained, "I'm not at all concerned about that, for I know the Lord is always on the side of right. But it's my constant anxiety and prayer that I and this nation should be on the Lord's side."

His anxiety must be ours. Or in the words of the old Jewish prayer:

From the conscience that shrinks from new truth
From the laziness that is content with half-truths
From the arrogance that thinks it knows all truths
O God of Truth
Deliver us.

Questions for Discussion

1. Should Christians be afraid to test the truthfulness of their beliefs? Discuss your answer in detail.
2. What attitudes are necessary in order to approach Jesus and His Word? Be specific.
3. According to David Lipscomb, what attitudes does a truth seeker possess?
4. Name the four stages of growth that religious movements undergo. Which stage do you feel best describes the twentieth century church?
5. Why are we satisfied to identify one another by tests of orthodoxy rather than orthopraxy?

6. Is it proper to make your explanation of Scripture as authoritative as Scripture? Explain your answer.
7. Name the seven essentials which constitute the faith.
8. How do you distinguish matters of opinion from matters of faith?
9. Should matters of opinion be made tests of fellowship? Explain your answer.

Endnotes

1. John Stuart Mill, *Philosophy History and Problems*, p. 471.

2. Dewey M. Beegle, *Scripture, Tradition and Infallibility*, (Ann Arbor: Pyor Pettengill, 1979), p. 19.

3. Bernard Ramm, *Protestant Biblical Interpretation*, (Grand Rapids: Baker Book House, 1970), p. 75

4. Thomas Campbell, "Declaration and Address," *Historical Documents Advocating Christian Union*, (Joplin: College Press, 1985), p. 116.

5. David Lipscomb, "Gospel Advocate," *I Just Want to Be a Christian*, (Nashville: Twentieth Century Christian), p. 157.

6. H. Paul Chalfant, *Religion in Contemporary Society*, (Sherman Oaks: Alfred Publishing Co., 1981), p. 111.

7. *Ibid.*, p. 111.

8. Barton W. Stone, *Christian Messenger*, (Vol. 9, No. 1, January 1835).

9. Thomas Campbell, *op. cit.*, p. 144.

12

the god of success

A few years ago, my oldest daughter and I went to the florist to pick up a Mother's Day arrangement. My daughter was given the task of holding the flowers in her lap so that they wouldn't tip over. She gladly accepted the responsibility. She tenderly held the arrangement with hands of love, singing all the way home.

Upon arrival, I parked the car in the garage. Jessica carefully got out of the car, still embracing the flowers; when she noticed a small white daisy petal on the front seat. Instantly her joy turned to disappointment. She looked at me with large sad eyes and said, "Daddy, I didn't do it." I reassured her that everything was O.K. "Mommy won't notice it anyway," I replied.

As we went into the house I thought about her attitude. Jessica was giving a gift of love to her mother and she wanted it to be perfect!

Mediocrity should have no place in the life of a Christian. We are bringing a gift to our heavenly Father and laying it on the altar. We are presenting our bodies as living sacrifices and, therefore, shouldn't be satisfied with anything short of our best (Rom. 12:1). This is the spirit of excellence.

SUCCESS IS RELATIVE

The Jews have a saying that God is more delighted in adverbs than in nouns. It's not so much what we do that is important, but rather how we do it; not how much, but how well. Those worshipping the god of success are preoccupied with performance; with the externals of "what" and "how much." Their watchword is, "Bigger and Better."

Man often judges the value of the person, or his work, by external indicators — and in some aspects, and to some degree, this may be appropriate. "By their fruits," said Jesus, "you will know them" (Matt. 7:20). However, externals are not always a clear indicator of internal realities. Judging success by externals can be misleading because success is relative.

Consider the parable of the talents as told by our Lord in Matthew 25:14-30. As the master prepares to leave for a long journey he distributes his wealth among his servants. One servant is apportioned five talents. Another servant is allotted two talents and still another, one talent. The master then leaves, trusting his servants to respond responsibly in their handling of his wealth.

After a long time the master returns. His servants are called into his office in order to settle the accounts. The man who had received five, as well as the man who had received two talents, doubled their money for the master. Both were highly commended for their faithfulness and foresight. The third man, however, hid his talent out of fear. He didn't lose, steal, or embezzle his master's funds. He simply gave back that which was given to him. The master criticized his laziness and lack of vision and fired the servant on the spot, casting him out of his fellowship.

The point of this parable is that God expects us to act in a responsible fashion with everything He gives to us, be it wealth, talents, time, etc. . . . It's God who makes us unique and different from one another. He is the source of our gifts and talents (I Cor. 4:7).

Let's retell the parable in a slightly different way, using success and not excellence as the standard of judgment.

Once there were three preachers, all called and equipped by God. To the first God bestowed five talents, to another, two; and to another, one. They all labored in different fields of service for their Master. The five-talent preacher labored in a large metropolitan congregation. He was surrounded by a number of energetic, evangelistic Christians who supported him in his ministry. Because of such support, he didn't need to actualize his own personal potential in order to maintain "respectable" growth. Therefore, at the end of the year this five-talent evangelist had eight talents to show for his labor.

The two-talent preacher worked in a small rural town called Podunk. He, like the five-talent preacher, loved his Master and labored faithfully in his field of service. He, on the other hand had little support from the congregation. But still he labored on. At the end of his year of service, this evangelist had four talents to return to his Master. The third preacher did exactly what the one-talent servant did in Jesus' parable and, therefore, he is of no concern to us.

Using success as the criteria of judgement, who will be judged most successful; the evangelist who finished with eight talents or the evangelist who finished with four? Obviously, success would say the man with eight. In fact, he doubled the output of the second man.

However, the ultimate question is, "Whom does God view as the most excellent evangelist?" God esteems the man with four talents as "excellent" because he maximized the talents that God had allotted to him. The man with eight talents was not as excellent because he was capable of producing ten.

Far too often the Lord's church uses success, and not excellence, as the standard of judgement. Overall, the eight-talent successful preacher will be the one in demand for the workshop circuit, and not the four-talent excellent preacher. God as my witness, I'm not being malicious — but you know that I'm right. I'm not excusing laziness or lack of growth. I am merely demonstrating the fact that the church can fall victim to the idol of success and fail to strive for excellence.

We must always remember that God calls the Christian to be faithful: not successful. We all long for the glorious ideal — to be a part of an exciting, evangelistic, expanding and intensely spiritual congregation. While I agree that the greatest churches have yet to be organized, and that we should strive to build such churches: the fact remains that faithfulness in less than ideal circumstances brings glory to God.

Consider the mission of God's prophet, Ezekiel. The Lord commissioned him to go and preach to the Jewish exiles who lived at Tel Aviv near the Kebar River. Not only was he commissioned to go to this particular place, but he was also told by the Lord Almighty that his audience would not listen; they would not respond.

No words could be more debilitating or depressing to a preacher. But to compound Ezekiel's burden, he was told that if God had chosen to send him to the Gentiles, "they

THE GOD OF SUCCESS

would have listened to you" (Ezek. 3:4-7). God deliberately sent Ezekiel to sow the word on rocky soil. Why? Because it served God's purpose. By worldly standards Ezekiel's ministry was not successful, but he was faithful to a difficult task. Therefore, in God's eyes, his ministry was excellent.

Consider the commission Jesus gave to the twelve in John chapter four. The disciples had just returned from town where they had purchased food for Jesus. The astonished disciples found their Master talking to a woman in public — a Samaritan woman at that! With great excitement this woman began telling the town's folk about Jesus and a crowd began to make its way toward the well where Jesus was seated.

As the cowd moved toward Him, Jesus directed the attention of His disciples toward the people with the words, "Open your eyes and look at the fields." The harvest time for these souls had arrived. Then Jesus tells the twelve:

> I sent you to reap that for which you have not labored; others have labored and you have entered into their labors (John 4:38).

The prophets of old had done the hard work with little visible results. It had been their task to clear the fields, break up the ground, prepare the soil and sow the seed. The disciples were now given the task of harvesting these souls into the kingdom. Jesus did not forget the less glorious ministries of the prophets. He realized that were it not for their faithful service in the face of discouraging circumstances, this harvest would not be possible. These prophets labored for centuries with this harvest as their goal; but they were not to be the ones to experience it. The apostle Paul reminds us of this principle when he says,

I planted, Apollos watered, but God gave the increase. So then neither he who plants is anything nor he who waters, but God who gives the increase. Now he who plants and he who waters are one, and *each one will receive his own reward according to his own labor* (I Cor. 3:6-8, Italics mine).

When it comes to evangelism we must always maintain a clear distinction between the part we play and the part God plays in the process of conversion.

While we must always remember that it is our responsibility to proclaim salvation, we must never forget that it is God who saves. . . . Our evangelistic work is the instrument that He uses for this purpose, but the power that saves is not in the instrument: it is in the hand of the One who uses the instrument. . . . If we regarded it as our job not simply to present Christ, but actually to produce converts — to evangelize, not only faithfully but successfully — our approach to evangelism would become pragmatic and calculating.[1]

Of course we want to be effective in our approach. We want to make the most of every opportunity (Eph. 5:15; Col. 4:5). We want to know how to answer everyone (Col. 4:6). Our task, however, is to sow the seed — lots of it! Pressure tactics, coercion, and manipulation come into play when we become success oriented. This temptation must be avoided.

A CALL TO EXCELLENCE

"And yet I show you a more excellent way." These words form the introduction to Paul's beautiful chapter in I

Corinthians concerning the absolute need for, and the character of love (I Cor. 13). Paul equates excellence with the practice of divine love. Therefore, when you find

> patience, kindness, a lack of envy, boasting or pride, respect rather than rudeness, concern for the well-being of others rather than self promotion, a lack of anger, an absence of grudges, a delight in the victories of others and not in their failures, a protective rather than divisive spirit, hope rather than despair, endurance and perseverance,

you have found Christian excellence. Where these attributes do not exist: excellence does not exist.

Paul's prayer for the Philippian saints was that their love, knowledge and discernment would abound so that they would be able to "approve the things that are excellent" (Phil. 1:10). Christians must be able to distinguish between things that differ. We are called to discipline our mind to think about things that are "true, noble, just, pure, lovely, virtuous, or excellent" (Phil. 4:8).

> The mind will always take on an order that conforms to the order of whatever it concentrates upon. . . . This is why the problem of mind pollution is so crucial. Now when I speak of mind pollution, I am not thinking only of "bad" books, movies and so forth but of the mediocre ones as well. You see, unless we set before ourselves an "habitual vision of greatness" we will surely degenerate.[2]

Success is limited to the few while excellence is attainable by all: but not without effort. We must not only desire excellence for the glory of God, but we must choose it as well. We must feed our minds with thoughts and concepts that will encourage the pursuit of excellence.

GOD — THE EPITOME OF EXCELLENCE

God can never be accused of shoddy workmanship. Mediocrity was never equated with His character. David joyfully proclaimed "O LORD our Lord, How excellent is your name in all the earth" (Psa. 8:1). Isaiah encourages us to sing to the LORD "for he has done excellent things" (Isa. 12:5). As His sons and daughters, shouldn't we demonstrate our Father's excellence in all we do?

What a person is gives meaning to all he does. Since we have been raised with Christ we should seek those things that are above (Col. 3:1). In Ephesians 2:8, Paul reminds us that we are God's workmanship; literally His masterpiece. As an artist's masterpiece reflects his excellence in his craft; so we are to reflect God's excellence in every facet of our lives.

Unbelievers form their opinions of God from what they see in us. Therefore, we should desire to be qualitatively different from the rest of mankind. The great violinist Isaac Stern was once asked by a reporter, "What truly distinguishes a great musician?" Stern replied, "A great musician is one who is always striving to improve, never content with his performances, always moving on to discover more about the instrument and the music he loves."[3] Every Christian, on a deeper level, must approach God with the same mind.

The great author, Robert Louis Stevenson, once shared this sobering thought with some young writers:

> Every piece of work which is not as good as you can make it, in which you have palmed off imperfect, meagerly thought, nominal in execution, upon mankind: every hasty or slovenly performance should rise up against you in the court of your own heart and condemn you for a thief.

How many times have you offered service to the Lord that was, "good enough"? It was said of Jesus that, "He has done all things well" (Mark 7:37). Wouldn't it be great if the world observed the same conscientious desire to reflect the Father's excellence in you and me? "Whatever you do, do all to the glory of God" (I Cor. 10:31).

Our love for God should be the motive for our excellence. "We love Him because He first loved us" (I John 4:19). A song that is commonly used to set the tone and to prepare our minds for the partaking of the Lord's supper is "When I Survey the Wondrous Cross." Isaac Watts, at a young age, realized that gratitude for salvation should be a compelling motive for excellence in all things.

> Were the whole realm of nature mine,
> That were a present far too small;
> Love so amazing, so divine,
> Demands my soul, my life, my all.[4]

CONCLUSION

Success is relative. That which appears successful to the world may not be excellent in the eyes of God. As we strive to reach a lost world for Jesus Christ, remember the love and patience He so excellently demonstrated in His ministry.

> A bruised reed he will not break,
> A smoking flax he will not quench
> (Matt. 12:20)

Success implies reaching certain external goals. Often, in order to reach these goals, integrity is compromised and

153

people are manipulated. If success is your god then the end justifies the means.

Excellence, on the other hand, is concerned with the means used to reach the end. Excellence deals with character, not performance. It focuses on who you are, rather than on what you do. Our God has done, and is doing, so much for us. Let's show Him our deep appreciation by living excellently in an age of mediocrity.

Questions for Discussion

1. Why should mediocrity have no place in the life of a Christian? Discuss your answer in detail.
2. Why is success relative? Use Matthew 25:14-30 in explaining your answer.
3. How does faithfulness in less than ideal circumstances bring glory to God?
4. Discuss the evangelistic principle Jesus mentions in John 4:38. Does the understanding of this principle change the way you view evangelism? If so, how?
5. According to Paul, what is a synonym for Christian excellence?
6. Discuss the concept of "mind pollution." How can the Christian avoid this?
7. Why should we be qualitatively different from the world?
8. What is the motive for our excellence?
9. How does Matthew 12:20 affect our attitude toward the weak? the lost?
10. How can evangelism become manipulative? Explain your answer.

Endnotes

1. J.I. Packer, *Evangelism and the Sovereignty of God*, (Downers Grove: InterVarsity Press, 1961), p. 27.

2. Richard Foster, *Study Guide for Celebration of Discipline*, (San Francisco: Harper and Row Publishers, 1983), p. 32.

3. Gary Inrig, *A Call to Excellence,* (Wheaton: Victor Books, 1985), p. 20.

4. Alton H. Howard, *Songs of the Church*, (West Monroe, 1977), p. 633.

13

the choice must be made

In the words of Solomon, "This is the end of the matter." The time has come to take action. We've briefly examined an entire Pandora's box of Satanic deceptions. We've identified the source of these pesky problems — the unregenerate heart. But knowledge alone is insufficient. Young people today are better educated and more well-informed concerning sexuality than past generations, but the teenage pregnancy rate continues to escalate at an alarming rate. Alcoholics go through treatment and are given the necessary tools to maintain sobriety, but they must choose to use this new knowledge and implement these steps. No one else can do it for them.

Truth will set you free only when you choose to act upon it — regardless of the personal cost or consequences. William Law (1686-1761) was a bitter opponent of Deism. In his classic work entitled *A Serious Call to a Devout and Holy Life,* he wrote:

If you will stop and ask yourselves why you are not as pious as the primitive Christians were, your own heart will tell you that it is neither though ignorance nor inability, but purely because you never thoroughly intended it.[1]

Our progress and growth in holiness depends upon God and ourselves — on God's grace and our will to be holy. We must have a real living determination to reach holiness.[2] We must be consumed with a zeal to be, think, and act like Christ. Though weak holiness may be accepted by God, it cannot, and must not, be chosen by us. We're not living a holy life if we choose to be weak. When you choose small holiness it becomes great unholiness in the eyes of our Creator.[3]

HOLINESS IS NOT STATIC

The Christian life is not static. It is an ever changing, ever enlarging, ever maturing relationship with Jesus Christ. The biblical writers express this progress in various ways. Paul wrote to the Church of God in Corinth, to those sanctified, or set apart[4] in Christ Jesus and called to be holy; or saints (I Cor. 1:2). In other words they've been set apart in a holy relationship and, therefore, must grow in that holiness. The Christian life unceasingly advances "from faith unto faith" (Rom. 1:17); from "one degree of glory to another" (II Cor. 3:18). Little by little, day by day, we should be looking more and more like Jesus.

Holiness implies an entire re-ordering of life. It is not merely a change in moral behavior. An individual can practice outward decency and retain an old empty heart (Matt. 12:43-45). Christianity is not merely practicing certain virtues and avoiding certain vices. Christianity is allowing God, through His Holy Spirit, to control all our actions and attitudes. Without such practical holiness no one, no matter how morally decent, will see the Lord (Heb. 12:14). Thankfully our Father knows the difference between falling short and stopping short of perfection. This is to be expected since holiness is progressive and not static.

> Though people will be admitted to heaven without reaching perfection, it does not follow that people will be admitted to heaven without striving for perfection. There is surely a great difference between falling short of perfection and stopping short of it.[5]

THE KINGDOM — PRESENTED FOR A DECISION

Every time Jesus offered the kingdom of heaven to man, He expected a decision to be made. To our Lord, there are only two camps in which we can stand — for Him or against Him; with Christ or with Anti-Christ; with the kingdom of God, or with the world.

Many members of the church, however, want to find a middle ground. They want to have the best of both worlds — to have their cake and eat it too. Leslie D. Weatherhead coined a New Beatitude, "Blessed are they who do not try to make the best of two worlds." These two-world people are not wicked enough to find happiness in their wickedness while at the same time they're not spiritual enough to find joy in the Lord. They become the epitome of grievous frustration.

When they're enjoying the "pleasures of sin" they feel guilty, defeated, and ashamed. When they're living for the Lord they cast an envious glance to the prosperous of this world, feeling like a martyr. They constantly feel the tug —

"damned if I do, damned if I don't." They feel this pull simply due to the fact that they have never decided which world they're going to live in. Perhaps you're going through this spiritual tug of war right now. If so — then it's time to make a choice.

True, Christianity, like radical surgery, is postponed as long as possible. No one enjoys going under the knife and no one enjoys making the radical choices that our Lord demands. He knowingly came not to pacify, but to bring the sword of decision (Matt. 10:34). The choice must be made. A refusal to choose is a refusal of Jesus and His Kingdom.

In the living laboratory of the concentration camps, Victor Frankl wrote:

> We watched and witnessed some of our comrades behave like swine while others behaved like saints. Man has both potentials within himself: which one is actualized *depends on decisions* but *not on conditions*. After all, man is that being who invented the gas chamber of Auschwitz: however, he is also that being who entered those gas chambers upright, with the Lord's Prayer or the Shema Yisrael on his lips.[6]

If we are to be conformed to the image of Christ we must make Him the exclusive focus in our life. We must fix our eyes on Jesus, the Pioneer and the Perfector of our faith (Heb. 12:2). We must love Him more than self, society, family or possessions (Luke 14:26f, 33). Only the consciousness of sin, and the realization of our own spiritual bankruptcy, can force us through the narrow gate of repentance — a gate which must be passed through daily (Luke 9:23).

Jesus will never force anyone to become a Christian and He will never force anyone to remain a Christian. Neither will He force anyone to grow as a Christian. Only you can choose to surrender your life into His loving hands. Just as only we can make the choice of conversion, so we only can make the choice for consecration. Far too often, however, church members choose the first and ignore the second. The result is our congregations are filled with lukewarm, worldly-minded, carnal believers and not fiery soldiers for the Lord (II Tim. 2:4).

The cross of Christ is not a dispensible luxury that we can do without. If God could have saved us in any other way, Calvary would not have taken place (Gal. 2:21). But it did. Therefore, the cross perpetually proclaims two powerful lessons. First, we are loved and highly valued by God (John 3:16). Secondly, at the cross we are forced to see the ugliness and horror of our own spiritual condition apart from God; for only deadly illnesses demand such radically drastic cures.

Jesus could not dispense with His cross and we cannot dispense with ours. We must voluntarily choose to carry it daily.

Stop for a moment and take a spiritual inventory. Ask yourself the following questions:

1. Spiritually, where have I been?
2. Where am I now?
3. What do I want to be for my Lord Jesus?
4. In what direction do I want my life to go?
5. What hindrances need to be removed or overcome in order to reach my desired destination?
6. Do I believe that God's spirit of power will enable me to break any bondage or defeat any sin?

God is for us, therefore, who or what can stand against us (Rom. 8:31)? He has bestowed upon us incomparably great power, a power greater than anything the world can muster against us (Eph. 1:18-20; I John 4:4). Therefore, we have no reason to continually grovel in weakness and mediocrity. The creative power of the universe is behind us!

There's only one way to release that power in your life. Commit all you have and all you are into the Father's hands (Luke 23:46). Decide to stop straddling the fence. Either Jesus is real to you or He is not. Either heaven is your home or it is not. Those who painfully try to make the best of two worlds find themselves not blessed, but cursed — both in this present world and in the one to come. They ultimately lose both. But if you freely surrender this world to Jesus — you'll obtain possession of the next, but the Lord also throws in the earth as well. In the first case this life becomes a foretaste of hell, in the second — a foretaste of heaven.

Which would you prefer? The choice is yours. After they had battled seven years for possession of the promised land, Joshua assembled the people to renew their dedication to God and His covenant. He challenged them with these words:

> And if it seems evil to you to serve the LORD, choose for yourselves this day whom you will serve, whether the gods which your fathers served that were on the other side of the River, or the gods of the Amorites, in whose land you dwell. But as for me and my house, we will serve the LORD (Josh. 24:15).

They had to make a decisive choice between the gods of the past, the gods of the present land in which they were dwelling, or the God who encompasses past, present and future. Although they had fought under Jehovah's banner for seven years, they had compromised their faith and were influenced by their surroundings.

They made a choice that day to reject all other gods and worship Jehovah God alone. It's my prayer that this book has encouraged you to do the same; that holiness will once again be the norm and not the exception; that the false gods of this world will be abandoned and the God of worlds without end will be adorned.

Questions for Discussion

1. Why are we not as pious as the first-century Christians?
2. Were all the first-century saints perfect models of Christianity? Use the Scriptures to support your answer.
3. Does the Christian ever arrive at perfection in this life?
4. Why do you feel that many Christians are frustrated in their walk with Christ? What's the solution?
5. What are two lessons which the cross of Christ teaches us?
6. How do I release the flow of God's power in my life?
7. What idols do you need to tear from your heart? What is the first step?
8. Why is the gift of "choice" such a phenomenal gift?
9. After completing this study, did you find the topics to be timely and of importance?
10. Would you recommend this book to others?

May the love of God, the grace of our Lord Jesus Christ, and the fellowship of the Holy Spirit be with you always.

Endnotes

1. William Law, *A Serious Call to a Devout and Holy Life*, (Nashville: The Upper Room).

2. Mother Teresa, *Christianity Today*, (November 20, 1987), p.45.

3. William Law, *Christian Perfection*, (Wheaton: Tyndale House, 1976), p.15

4. The Greek root of the word sanctified is the same root as the word holy.

5. William Law, *Christian Perfection*, (Wheaton: Tyndale House, 1976), p.15

6. Victor E. Frankl, *Man's Search For Meaning*, (New York: Washington Square Press, 1984), p. 157.